cute & easy
crochet

cute & easy crochet

Learn to crochet with these 35 adorable projects

Nicki Trench

CICO BOOKS
LONDON NEW YORK

Published in 2011 by CICO Books
an imprint of Ryland Peters & Small Ltd
20-21 Jockey's Fields, London WC1R 4BW

www.cicobooks.com

10

A CIP catalogue record for this book is available from the
British Library.

ISBN 978 1 907563 06 5

Printed in China

Editor: Marie Clayton
Designer: Christine Wood
Photographer: Penny Wincer
Stylist: Alison Davidson. Additional styling by
Rose Hammick.

Contents

Introduction

I'm delighted by the latest enthusiasm for crochet and *Cute & Easy Crochet* aims to inspire and meet with current trends to entice and feed all levels with great patterns and designs.

Modern colours and yarns have transformed crochet and shaken off any negative reputation. The granny square has emerged with glorious colours and luxurious crochet pieces have swamped the high streets with pretty scarves, cool dresses and elegant wraps.

Crochet has now established itself as a popular contemporary craft with people flocking to classes to learn this traditional skill that has somehow missed a generation, while the previous generations took it for granted as a handed-down knowledge.

In *Cute & Easy Crochet*, we've divided the projects into chapters that cover the various skill groups: Starting Out for the Beginner, Practice Makes Perfect for Improvers and Confident Crocheting for Enthusiasts. We've used up-to-date wools and simple designs that will inspire you whatever your level; there is something in *Cute & Easy Crochet* for all. Beginners will love the easy projects in Starting Out that need only the basic skills and stitches; see the gorgeous Rose Shopper (page 40), the Round Stripy Cushion Cover (page 32) or try the stunning Springtime Throw made of lots of little easy squares (page 24).

Once you've gathered confidence, the Practice Makes Perfect projects start to introduce edgings and a little more intricate pattern reading, while still keeping things simple. See the Chunky Seashell Scarf (page 68) or the cosiest gloves you've ever seen (page 74).

The Confident Crochet section is for those enthusiasts who are very comfortable reading patterns and have mastered and practiced the basic techniques. You won't be able to resist the Babushkas (page 96), the Summer Evening Shawl (page 112) or the blanket made with my favourite squares: Camellia Blanket (page 88).

If you're making for a baby, we have some lovely designs and easy projects: Baby Blanket (page 66), Baby Slippers (page 84) and the delightful teddies, Monty and Priscilla (page 120). If you'd like to make an original gift, try the brilliant Baby Bibs (page 82).

Cute & Easy Crochet has an excellent Crochet Know-how section with clear illustrations that will show you exactly how to master the techniques used in the patterns. Don't be put off by crochet abbreviations – they are really easy to master and explained in each pattern.

As soon as I was commissioned to write this book, I immediately rushed to my local haberdashery and bought ribbons and trimmings to use as my colour palette guide. I hope the light blues, yellows, pinks, greens and lilacs will evoke the atmosphere of spring and summer, even if you're crocheting in the middle of winter in front of the fire.

Crochet know-how

Techniques

In this section, we explain how to master the simple crochet techniques that you need to make the projects in this book.

Making a slip knot

The simplest way is to make a circle with the yarn, so that the loop is facing downwards.

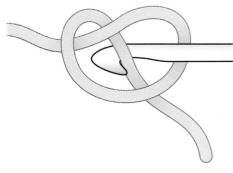

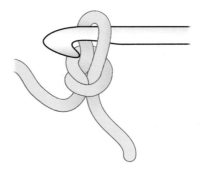

1 In one hand hold the circle at the top, where the yarn crosses, and let the tail drop down so that it falls in the centre of the loop. With your free hand or the tip of a crochet hook, pull the tail through the loop and pull the knot, so that it tightens loosely.

2 Put the hook into the circle and pull the knot gently so that it forms a loose loop on the hook.

Holding the hook

Pick up your hook as though you were picking up a pen or pencil. Keeping the hook held loosely between your fingers and thumb, turn your hand that so the palm is facing up and the hook is balanced in your hand and resting in the space between your index finger and your thumb.

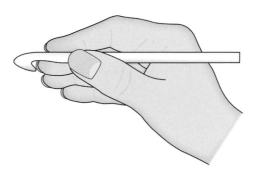

Holding yarn

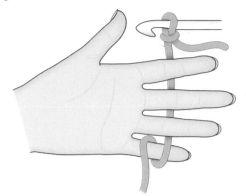

Pick up the yarn with your little finger in the opposite hand to your hook, with your palm facing upwards. Turn your hand to face downwards, with the yarn on top of your index finger and under the other two fingers and wrapped right around the little finger. Keeping your index finger only at a slight curve, hold your work just under the slip knot with the other hand.

Yarn around hook

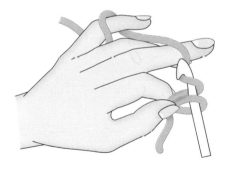

To create a stitch, you'll need to catch the yarn with the hook and pull it through the loop. Holding your yarn and hook correctly, catch the yarn from behind with the hook pointed upwards. As you gently pull the yarn through the loop on the hook, turn the hook so that it faces downwards and slide the yarn through the loop. The loop on the hook should be kept loose enough so that the hook slides through easily.

Chain

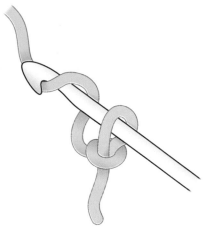

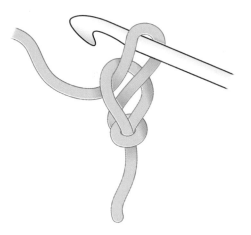

1 Using the hook, wrap the yarn around the hook and pull it through the loop on the hook, creating a new loop on the hook. Continue in this way to create a chain of the required length.

2 Keep moving your middle finger and thumb close to the hook, to hold the work in place with the opposite hand that you hold your hook with.

Chain ring/circle

If you are crocheting a round shape, one way of starting off is by crocheting a number of chains following the instructions in your pattern, and then joining them into a circle.

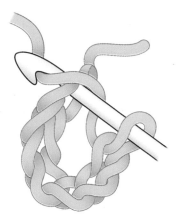

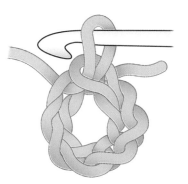

Some of the circles in this book have been made by creating a spiral, whereby you make two chains and insert your hook into the second chain from the hook (the first chain you made). Following the instructions in the pattern will then ensure the spiral has the correct amount of stitches. It's essential to use a stitch marker when using this method, so that you know where to start and finish your round.

1 To join the chain into a circle, insert the crochet hook into the first chain that you made (not into the slip knot), yarn around hook, then pull the yarn through the chain and through the loop on your hook at the same time, thereby creating a slip stitch and forming a circle.

2 You will now have a circle ready according to your pattern.

Chain space

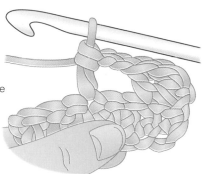

1 A chain space (ch sp) is the space that has been made under a chain in the previous round or row and falls in between other stitches.

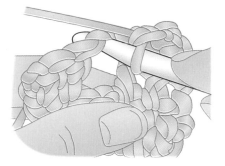

2 Stitches into a chain space are made directly into the hole created under the chain and not into the chain stitches themselves.

Marking rounds

Place a stitch marker at the beginning of each round; a piece of yarn in a contrasting colour is useful for this. Loop the stitch marker into the first stitch; when you have made a round and reached the point where the stitch marker is, work this stitch, take out the stitch marker from the previous round and put it back into the first stitch of the new round.

Slip stitch

A slip stitch doesn't create any height and is often used as the last stitch to create a smooth and even round or row.

1 To make a slip stitch: put the hook through the work, yarn around hook.

2 Pull the yarn through both the work and through the loop on the hook at the same time.

Double crochet

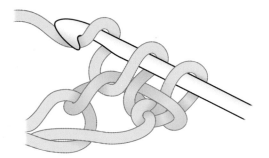

1 Insert the hook into your work, yarn around hook and pull the yarn through the work. You will then have two loops on the hook.

2 Yarn around hook again and pull through the two loops on the hook. You will then have one loop on the hook.

Half treble

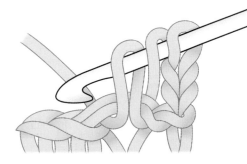

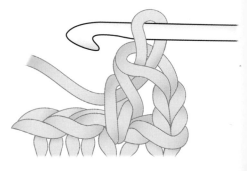

1 Before inserting the hook into the work, wrap the yarn around the hook and put the hook through the work with the yarn wrapped around.

2 Yarn around hook again and pull through the first loop on the hook (you now have three loops on the hook).

3 Yarn around hook and pull the yarn through all three loops. You'll be left with one loop on the hook.

Treble

1 Before inserting the hook into the work, wrap the yarn around the hook and put the hook through the work with the yarn wrapped around.

2 Yarn around hook again and pull through the first loop on the hook (you now have three loops on the hook). Yarn around hook again, pull the yarn through two loops (you now have two loops on the hook).

3 Pull the yarn through two loops again. You will be left with one loop on the hook.

Double treble

Yarn around hook twice, insert hook into the stitch, yarn around hook, pull a loop through (four loops on hook), yarn around hook, pull the yarn through two stitches (three loops on hook), yarn around hook, pull a loop through the next two stitches (two loops on hook), yarn around hook, pull a loop through the last two stitches.

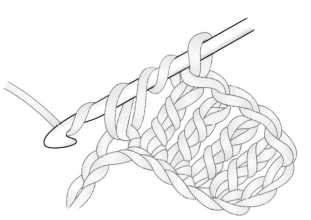

Triple treble

Yarn around hook three times, insert hook into the stitch, yarn around hook, pull a loop through (five loops on hook), yarn around hook, pull the yarn through two stitches (four loops on hook), yarn around hook, pull a loop through the next two stitches (three loops on hook), yarn around hook, pull a loop through the next two stitches (two loops on hook), yarn around hook, pull a loop through the last two stitches.

Making rows

When making straight rows, you need to make a turning chain at the end to create the height you need for the stitch you're working with. To do this, you just make the right number of chains for the stitch you are working in as follows:

Double crochet = 1 chain
Half treble crochet = 2 chain
Treble crochet = 3 chain
Double treble crochet = 4 chain

Joining new yarn

If using double crochet, insert the hook as normal into the stitch, using the original yarn, and pull a loop through. Drop the old yarn and pick up the new yarn. Wrap the new yarn around the hook and pull it through the two loops on the hook.

Decreasing

You can decease by either missing the next stitch and continuing to crochet, or by crocheting two or more stitches together. The basic technique is the same no matter which stitch you are using; the illustration shows working three trebles (tr3tog) in progress:

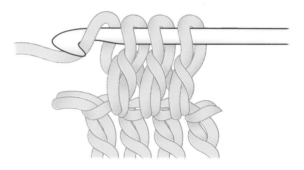

Work a treble into each of the next three stitches as normal, but leave the last loop of each stitch on the hook (four loops on the hook). Yarn around hook and pull the yarn through all the stitches on the hook to join them together. You will finish with one loop on the hook.

Increasing

Make two or three stitches into one stitch from the previous row. The illustration shows a two-stitch increase being made.

Double crochet two stitches together

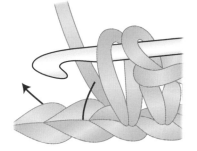

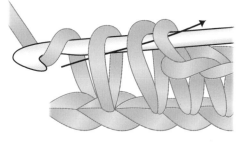

1 Insert hook into next stitch, draw a loop through, insert hook into next stitch.

2 Draw a loop through, yarn around hook and pull through all three stitches.

Half treble two stitches together

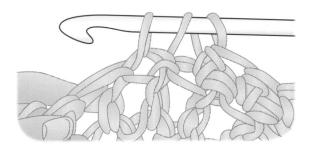

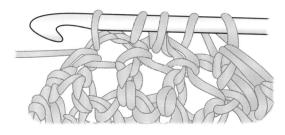

1 Yarn around hook, insert hook into next stitch, yarn around hook, draw yarn through (three loops on hook).

2 Yarn around hook, insert hook into next stitch, yarn around hook, draw yarn through.

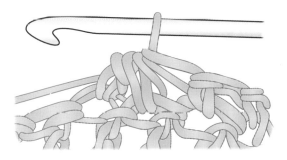

3 Draw yarn through all five loops on hook.

How to double crochet squares together

Place two squares wrong sides together, lining them up so that the stitches on each square match. Put the hook through the top loops of the first square and also through the corresponding top loops of the second square. Join in the yarn, make 1 chain, insert the hook into the top stitches of both squares and make a double crochet seam across the top of the squares.

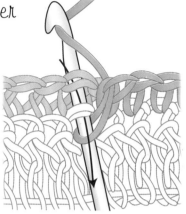

Cluster

Yarn around hook, insert hook into next stitch, pull yarn through work, yarn around hook, insert hook into same stitch, pull yarn through work, yarn around hook, insert hook into same stitch, pull yarn through work. Pull yarn through all seven loops on hook, 1 chain.

Fastening off

Cut the yarn leaving a tail of approx 10cm (4in). Pull the tail all the way through the loop.

chapter 1

Starting out

Springtime Throw

This is a delightful project and the squares are very easy and perfect for a beginner. It's the colours of the Rooster yarn that make this so special – but it also works well using scraps of yarn.

level 1: Beginner

materials
Rooster Almerino DK (50% baby alpaca, 50% merino wool)
21 x 50g balls (2362.5m/2604yds) 201 Cornish (MC)
5 x 50g balls (562.5m/620yds) each of:
209 Smoothie
207 Gooseberry
203 Strawberry Cream
2205 Glace
204 Grape
210 Custard
4mm (F/5) crochet hook

abbreviations
ch chain
ch sp chain space
dc double crochet
rep repeat
ss slip stitch
st(s) stitch(es)
tr treble
WS wrong side

finished measurement
Approx 162 x 223cm (64 x 88in)

tension
Tension is not critical on this project.

method

Make 432 squares in total: 14 each of 30 different colour combinations (420 squares), plus another 12 random colourways. On every square, Round 2 is made using MC.

square

Using first colour, make a loop, then make 4ch. Join with ss into first ch to form a ring.

Round 1: 3ch, 2tr into ring, 2ch, 3tr into ring, 2ch, *3tr into ring, 2ch; rep from * once more.
Ss into top of first 3ch.
Fasten off.
Place hook through a ch sp and join in MC.

Round 2: 3ch, 2tr, 3ch, 3tr into same ch sp (first corner), 2ch, *3tr, 3ch, 3tr into next ch sp, 2ch; rep from * twice more.
Ss into top of first 3ch.
Fasten off.
Put hook into top of fastened-off stitch, join in third colour, make 1ch.

Round 3: 1dc into top of next 2 sts, 3dc into next ch sp, 1dc into top of next 3 sts, 2dc into next ch sp, *1dc into top of next 3 sts, 3dc into next ch sp, 1dc into top of next 3 sts, 2dc into next ch sp; rep from * twice more.
Ss into top of first ch.
Fasten off.
Sew in ends neatly and securely after making each square.

to make up

Lay out the squares with 18 squares across (width) by 24 squares down (length) in a random order. Using MC and with WS together, join squares first in horizontal rows and then in vertical rows, using a dc seam. When all squares are joined, work one row of dc edging all the way around blanket. When turning corners, make 2dc, 1ch, 2dc into each corner stitch.
Fasten off.
Sew in ends.

tip

This is a large blanket and takes up a lot of balls of yarn. It's made up from lots of small squares, so it's very easy to adjust the sizing by making fewer or more squares; just remember to adjust the yarn quantities.

Knickerbockerglory Bunting

Bunting evokes all the atmosphere of spring and summer, whatever the weather and wherever you hang it. It's a lovely, happy way to brighten up a child's room, a garden, kitchen, hallway or just about anywhere at all.

level 1: Beginner

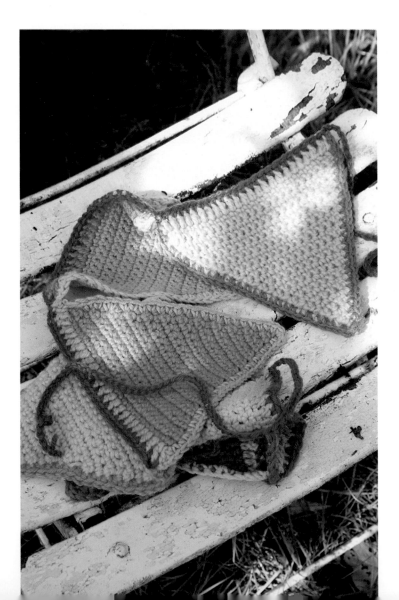

materials

King Cole Merino Blend DK (100% merino wool)
1 x 50g ball (112m/123yds) each of:
5 Sky
55 Gold
94 Dusky Pink
787 Fuchsia
Debbie Bliss Cashmerino DK (55% merino wool, 33% microfibre, 12% cashmere)
1 x 50g ball (110m/120yds) each of:
017 Lilac
029 Light green
Rowan Belle Organic DK (50% organic wool, 50% cotton)
1 x 50g ball (120m/131yds) 004 Persimmon
4mm (F/5) crochet hook
Yarn sewing needle

abbreviations

ch chain
dc double crochet
dc2tog Insert hook into next st, draw a loop through, insert hook into next st, draw a loop through, pull through all 3 sts
rep repeat
RS right side
ss slip stitch
st(s) stitch(es)
tr treble

finished measurement
Each flag approx 18cm (7in) across top

tension
Tension is not critical on this project.

method
Make 6, or as many as required, in different colours with contrast edgings.

flag
Using flag main colour, make 26ch.
Row 1: 1dc in 2nd ch from hook, 1dc in each ch to end. (*25 sts*)
Row 2: 1ch, dc2tog, 1dc in each st to end.
Rep Row 2 until 2 sts remain, dc2tog.
Fasten off.

edging
With RS facing, join in first contrast colour into top right corner st, 3ch, make 24tr along top edge.
Fasten off.

With RS facing, join next contrast colour in top left corner, 1ch, work 26dc along first side, 3dc in corner st, 26dc along other side ending with a ss into top of first treble.
Fasten off.
Sew in ends.

to make up
With contrasting col, make 70ch. With RS facing, join ch to first flag with ss in right-hand corner, 1ch, *1dc in between each tr across top of flag to end, join next flag with ss into top right-hand corner; rep from * to end for each flag, ss into last corner st of last flag. Make 70ch. Fasten off.

Using a tapestry needle at back of work, stitch to secure joins in between each flag using loose ends of wool. Sew in ends well. Press each flag.

> **tips**
> If you'd like to stiffen your flags, try using a little starch before hanging.
>
> Making bunting out of your odds and ends of wool is ideal and a great way to use up spare wool left over from other projects.
>
> I have chosen colours from different brands to get the yummy colour scheme – just make sure the yarn is a similar weight.

Hook Holder

This is such a handy little tool kit and great for keeping your crochet hooks in. The spacing instructions here give you room for 12 hooks; just sew more lines into the lining for more hook spaces.

level 1: Beginner

materials

Rooster Almerino DK (50% baby alpaca, 50% merino wool)
1 x 50g ball (112.5m/124yds) each of:
210 Custard (A)
204 Grape (B)
4mm (F/5) crochet hook
23 x 33cm (9 x 13in) fabric for main lining
18 x 33cm (7 x 13in) fabric for pocket lining
1m (39in) x 1.5cm (⅝in) wide ribbon
Sewing needle and thread

abbreviations

ch chain
dc double crochet
rep repeat
RS right side
ss slip stitch
st(s) stitch(es)
WS wrong side

finished measurement

29 x 20cm (11½ x 8in)

tension

Tension is not critical on this project.

method

Using A, make 33ch.
Row 1: 1dc in next ch from hook and in every ch to end. (*32 sts*)
Rep Row 1 until work measures 29cm (11½in).
Fasten off.

edging

With RS facing and using B, make 58dc along one long edge, turn.
Next row: 1dc into first st, *3ch, ss into third ch from hook, miss 1 st, 1dc; rep from * to end.
Fasten off.
Rep on opposite long edge.
Fasten off.
Block and steam work.
When working on the main crochet piece from here on, the longest side becomes the width of the hook roll holder and the shorter side becomes the height.

lining

Measure the crochet piece, adding 1.5cm (⅝in) to each side for hem allowances, and cut the main lining fabric to size. Pin and press under a 1.5cm (⅝in) hem to the WS on each side, and machine stitch. Sew the top edge hem using a zigzag stitch.

Cut the pocket lining piece to the same width but 7.5cm (3in) shorter. Pin and press under a 1.5cm (⅝in) hem to the WS on all edges.

With RS of both pieces facing upwards, pin pocket lining to main lining, matching bottom edges and leaving an approx 7.5cm (3in) gap at the top. Sew pocket lining to main lining along the two short sides and the bottom edge, leaving the top open. To create the hook pockets, sew vertical lines down the pocket lining at approx 2.5cm (1in) intervals. Pin the whole lining piece to the wrong side of the crochet piece. Cut ribbon length in half. Insert approx 2.5cm (1in) of one ribbon piece halfway down the left-hand side, between the lining and main crochet piece.

to make up

With WS together, hand stitch the lining onto the crochet piece, incorporating the end of the ribbon. Starting from the short side opposite the ribbon, roll up the case. Pin and sew the other ribbon end onto hook piece to correspond with first ribbon end.

Floral Purse

This is a really easy and pretty purse to make and a great beginner's project, which takes only a small amount of time to achieve maximum effect.

level 1: Beginner

materials
Debbie Bliss Cashmerino Aran (55% merino wool, 33% microfibre, 12% cashmere)
1 x 50g ball (90m/98yds) 011 Green (MC)
Small lengths of DK yarn in pinks, purples, blues and yellow for flowers
4.5mm (G/6) and 4mm (F/5) crochet hooks
Yarn sewing needle
25.5 x 30.5cm (10 x 12in) lining fabric
Sewing needle and thread
1 x 1cm (½in) button

abbreviations
ch chain
ch sp chain space
dc double crochet
htr half treble
rep repeat
RS right side
ss slip stitch
st(s) stitch(es)
tr treble
WS wrong side

special abbreviations
htr2tog Yarn around hook, insert hook into next st, yarn around hook, draw a loop through, insert hook into next st, draw a loop through, yarn around hook and pull through all 4 loops.

finished measurement
Approx 15 x 10cm (6 x 4in)

tension
Tension is not critical on this project.

method
Using MC and 4.5mm (G/6) crochet hook, make 24ch.
Row 1: 1htr into second ch from hook, 1htr in each ch to end, 2ch, turn. (*22 sts – 2ch counts as first htr*)
Row 2: 1htr into each st, 2ch, turn.
Rep Row 2 until work measures approx 19cm (7½in).

Make flap:
Rows 1–4: 2ch, htr2tog, 1htr in each st to end. (*18 sts*)
Rows 5–7: 2ch, htr2tog, 1htr to last 2 sts, htr2tog. (*12 sts*)

Make buttonhole:
Row 1: 2ch, htr2tog, 1htr in each of next 2 sts, 2ch, miss 2 sts, 1htr in each of next 3 sts, htr2tog.
Row 2: 2ch, htr2tog, 1htr in next st, 2htr in ch sp, 1htr in next 3 sts. (*8 sts*)

Work edging:
Turn and make 32dc sts along first side, 3dc into corner st, 22dc sts along bottom edge, 3dc into corner st, 32dc sts along second side.
Fasten off.

flowers (make 4)
Use two colours for each flower.
Using first colour and 4mm (F/5) hook, 6ch, join with a ss into first ch.
Make 16dc into circle, joining tail around into each st, join with a ss.
Fasten off.
Join second colour into fastened-off st.
*3ch, make 1tr into next two sts, 3ch, ss into next st; rep from * 4 more times. (*5 petals*)
Fasten off.
Pull tail to close up centre hole and sew in ends.

lining
Block crocheted piece. Cut a piece of lining fabric the same size and shape of the purse, plus an extra 1.5cm (⅝in) hem allowance all round. Pin, press and machine or hand sew hems of lining. Match up buttonhole position on crocheted piece and make a buttonhole on lining to correspond.

to make up
With RS facing upwards, pin lining to WS of crocheted piece. Hand stitch in place, ensuring that the buttonholes match up. With RS of lining facing, turn bottom edge up to start of flap (decrease sides). Using yarn, sew side seams of purse, leaving the flap open. Sew on button to correspond with buttonhole. Sew three flowers to front and one to back of purse.

Round Stripy Cushion Cover

Crochet is perfect for making circles and this cushion cover is a project I've been teaching to all my beginner students for many years, because it is beautiful and easy to make. It uses simple treble stitch and the gorgeous range of Amy Butler colours from Rowan Yarns.

level 1: Beginner

materials

Rowan Belle Organic Aran (50% organic wool, 50% cotton)
1 x 50g ball (90m/98yds) each of:
209 Robin's Egg (A)
203 Orchid (B)
205 Rose (C)
212 Zinc (D)
206 Poppy (E)
211 Cilantro (F)
5mm (H/8) crochet hook
40cm (16in) round cushion pad

abbreviations

ch chain
cont continue
dc double crochet
ss slip stitch
tr treble
WS wrong side

finished measurement

To fit a 40cm (16in) diameter cushion pad

tension

14tr x 8 rows over a 10cm (4in) square, using 5mm (H/8) hook.

method (make 2 sides)

Using A, make 6ch, join with ss into first ch.
Round 1: 3ch (counts as first tr), 11tr into circle, join with a ss into top of first 3-ch.
Change to B.
Round 2: 3ch, 1tr into same st, 2tr into every st to end of round, join with a ss into top of first 3-ch. (24 sts)
Change to C.
Round 3: 3ch, 1tr into same st, * 1tr into next st, 2tr into next 2 sts; rep from * to last 2 sts, 1tr into next st, 2tr into last st, join with a ss into top of first 3-ch. (40 sts)
Change to D.
Round 4: 3ch, 1tr into same st, * 1tr into next 3 sts, 2tr into next st; rep from *to last 3 sts, 1tr into each of last 3 sts, join with a ss into top of first 3-ch. (50 sts)
Change to E.
Round 5: 3ch, 1tr into same st, * 1tr into next 4 sts, 2tr into next st; rep from * to last 4 sts, 1tr into each of last 4 sts, join with ss into top of first 3-ch. (60 sts)
Change to F.
Round 6: 3ch, 1tr into same st, * 1tr into next 5 sts, 2tr into next st; rep from *to last 5 sts, 1tr into each of last 5 sts, join with a ss into top of first 3-ch. (70 sts)
Change to A.
Round 7: 3ch, 1tr into same st, * 1tr into next 6 sts, 2tr into next st; rep from * to last 6 sts, 1tr into each of last 6 sts, join with a ss into top of first 3-ch. (80 sts)
Change to B.
Round 8: 3ch, 1tr into same st, * 1tr into next 7 sts, 2tr into next st; rep from *to last 7 sts, 1tr into each of last 7 sts, join with a ss into top of first 3-ch. (90 sts)
Change to C.
Round 9: 3ch, 1tr into same st, * 1tr into next 8 sts, 2tr into next st; rep from * to last 8 sts, 1tr into each of last 8 sts, join with a ss into top of first 3-ch. (100 sts)
Change to D.
Round 10: As Round 5. (120 sts)
Change to E.
Round 11: 3ch, 1tr into same st, * 1tr into next 11 tr, 2tr in next st; rep from * to last 11 tr, 1tr in each of last 11 tr, join with a ss into top of first 3-ch. (130 sts)
Change to F.
Round 12: 3ch, 1tr into same st, * 1tr into next 12 tr, 2tr in next st; rep from *

to last 12 tr, 1tr into last 12 tr, join with a ss into top of first 3-ch.
Change to A.
Round 13: As Round 7.
Change to B.
Round 14: 3ch, 1tr into same st, * 1tr into next 15 tr, 2tr in next st, rep from *
to last 15 tr, 1tr in each of last 15 tr, join with a ss into top of first 3-ch.
Change to C.
Round 15: 3ch, 1tr into same st, * 1tr into next 16 tr, 2tr in next st; rep from *
to last 16 tr, 1tr in each of last 16 tr, join with a ss into top of first 3-ch.
Change to D.
Round 16: As Round 9.

to make up
Put cushion sides WS facing. Insert
hook into both sides and, using A,
make 1ch. Make 1dc into each st,
putting hook through both sides and
joining sides together, leaving a big
enough gap to push through cushion
pad. Cont in dc until seam is fully
joined together.
Fasten off. Sew in ends.

Beanie Hat

This hat has a really good shape, so it looks good either with or without the flower. It will also work for both men and women.

level 2: Improver

materials
Rooster Almerino Aran (50% baby alpaca, 50% merino wool)
2 x 50g balls (188m/206yds) each of:
309 Ocean (A)
307 Brighton Rock (B)
4mm (F/5) crochet hook
Yarn sewing needle

abbreviations
ch chain
ch sp chain space
dc double crochet
htr half treble
st(s) stitch(es)
ss slip stitch

special abbreviations
cl (cluster) Yarn around hook, insert hook into ch or st, pull yarn through work, yarn around hook, insert hook into same ch, pull yarn through work, yarn around hook, insert hook into same ch, pull yarn through work, pull yarn through all 7 loops on hook, 1ch.
htr2tog Yarn around hook, insert hook into next st, yarn around hook, draw a loop through, insert hook into next st, draw a loop through, yarn around hook and pull through all 4 loops.

finished measurement
To fit an average adult head

tension
Tension is not critical on this project.

method

Using A, make 86ch, ss into first ch to form a ring.

Round 1: 1ch, 1dc in each ch to end, ss into first ch.

Rounds 2–5: 1ch, 1dc in each st to end, ss into first ch.

Rounds 6–9: 2ch, 1htr in each st to end, ss into first 2-ch.

Round 10: *1cl in next st, 1ch, miss 1 st; rep from * to end, ss into top of first cl.

Round 11: 2ch, * 1htr in top of cl, 1htr in next ch sp; rep from * to end, ss into first 2ch.

Round 12: 2ch, 1htr in each st to end, ss into first 2-ch.

Round 13: 2ch, *1htr in next 4 sts, htr2tog; rep from * to end, ss into first 2-ch.

Round 14: 2ch, 1htr in each st to end, ss into first 2-ch.

Round 15: Miss 1 st, *1cl in next st, 1ch, miss 1 st; rep from * to end.

Round 16: 2ch, *1htr in top of cl, 1htr in ch sp; rep from * to end, ss into first 2-ch.

Round 17: 2ch, *1htr in next 3 sts, htr2tog; rep from * to end, ss into first 2-ch.

Round 18: 2ch, *1htr in each st to end, ss into first 2-ch.

Round 19: Rep Round 18.

Round 20: 2ch, *1htr in next 2 sts, htr2tog; rep from * to end, ss into first 2-ch.

Round 21: 2ch, 1htr in each st to end, ss into first 2-ch.

Round 22: 2ch, *1htr in next st, htr2tog; rep from * to end, ss into first 2-ch.

Round 23: Rep Round 21.

Round 24: 2ch, *htr2tog; rep from * to end, ss into first 2-ch.

Round 25: 2ch, 1htr in each st to end, ss into first 2-ch.

Fasten off, leaving a long tail.

flower

Using B, make 54ch.

Row 1: 1tr into 5th ch from hook, * 1ch, miss 1ch, (1tr, 1ch, 1tr) in next ch; rep from * to end.

Row 2: 3ch, 5tr in first ch sp, *1dc in next ch sp, 6tr in next ch sp; rep from *, ending with 6tr in last ch sp. (*25 shells*)

Fasten off, leaving a long tail for sewing flower together.

to make up

To finish hat, thread tail onto a yarn sewing needle, thread through remaining stitches and pull tightly, sew in end.

To finish flower, thread needle with yarn tail and weave down side of shell to bottom. Roll first shell tightly to form centre bud. Work two stitches at base of shell to hold in place. Roll remaining strip around bud to form flower, securing as you roll by stitching through layers of chains at bottom of flower. Sew flower onto side of hat.

Patchwork Bag

This bag is made up of simple squares joined together to make a front, back, sides and bottom. It's a good size and is made using the lovely colour palette from Belle, the Amy Butler range of Rowan organic wool.

level 2: Improver

materials

Rowan Belle Organic DK (50% organic wool, 50% cotton)
3 x 50g balls (360m/393yds) 005 Basil (MC)
1 x 50g ball (120m/131yds) each of:
002 Cornflower
008 Peony
012 Tomato
009 Hibiscus
014 Robin's Egg
016 Cilantro
013 Moonflower
4mm (F/5) crochet hook
Yarn sewing needle
75 x 100cm (30 x 40in) piece of lining fabric
10 x 92cm (4 x 36in) piece of fusible interfacing
Sewing needle and thread

abbreviations

ch chain
ch sp chain space
cont continue
dc double crochet
RS right side
st(s) stitch(es)
ss slip stitch
tr treble
WS wrong side

finished measurement

Approx 30 x 30cm (12 x 12in)

tension

Tension is not critical on this project.

method

squares (make 27)
Use different colour combinations and change colour for each round, always using MC for Rounds 4 and 5.
Using first colour, 4ch, join with a ss.
Round 1: 3ch (counts as 1tr), 2tr into ring, *1ch, 3tr into ring; rep from * twice more, 1ch, ss into top of first 3ch.
Fasten off.
Round 2: Join 2nd colour into fastened-off st, make ss into each of next 2 tr and next 1ch sp, 3ch, 4tr into same sp to make a corner, *1tr into top centre st of next 3-tr group, 5tr into next ch sp to make another corner; rep from * twice more, 1tr into top centre st of next 3-tr group, ss to top of 3ch.
Fasten off.
Round 3: Join 3rd colour into top of centre st of any corner group, 3ch, 5tr into same place to make corner, *3tr into top st of next single tr, 6tr into top centre st of next corner group; rep from * twice, 3tr into top st of next single tr, ss to top of 3ch.
Fasten off.
Round 4: Join MC between 3rd and 4th tr of any corner group, 3ch, 5tr into same place for corner, *3tr in next sp, 3tr in next sp, 6tr into centre of next corner group; rep from * twice more, 3tr in next sp, 3tr in next sp, ss to top of 3-ch. Do not fasten off.
Round 5: Cont in MC, 1ch, 1dc in top of next 2 sts, 3dc in next st, *1dc in next 11 sts, 3dc; rep from * twice more, 1dc in next 9 sts, ss to top of first dc.
Fasten off.

to make up

Using a dc seam, attach squares together. Make two panels (front and back) of 3 x 3 squares. Add three squares down each side of one set. Join to other set, leaving one seam open. Join three squares across at the bottom of one set to form the base of the bag. Join these three squares to other panel and base of sides.

Rose Shopper

This easy, quick project, using double crochet throughout, is perfect as a shopper. The lining makes it stronger, but if you are not so handy at sewing, it still works brilliantly without one. The flowers are Improver level, so if these are above your skill, replace with some simple flowers from the Floral Purse – see page 30.

level 1: Beginner – shopper
level 2: Improver – flowers

materials

Debbie Bliss Como (90% wool, 10% cashmere)
6 x 50g balls (252m/276yds) 24 Silver (A)
1 x 50g ball (42m/46yds) 18 Lime (B)
Rowan Belle Organic DK (50% organic wool, 50% cotton)
1 x 50g ball (120m/131yds) 004 Persimmon (C)
Rooster Almerino Aran (50% baby alpaca, 50% merino wool)
1 x 50g ball (94m/103yds) 306 Gooseberry (D)
9mm (M/13), 7mm (K10½), and 4.5mm (G/6) crochet hooks
Yarn sewing needle
1m (19.5in) length of lining fabric for bag
72 x 15cm (28 x 5in) piece of lining fabric for handles
Sewing needle and thread
1 large press stud

abbreviations

ch chain
cont continue
dc double crochet
rep repeat
RS right side
st(s) stitch(es)
ss slip stitch
tr treble
WS wrong side

finished measurement

Shopper approx 34 x 29cm (13½ x 11½in), handles 64cm (25in)

tension

Tension is not critical on this project.

Fabric Seat Covers

These make great seat covers; they are worked with a giant crochet hook and strips of fabric joined together and take no time at all.

level 1: Beginner

materials
Approx 64m (70yds) x 2.5cm (1in) fabric strip wound into 2 x 500g balls
Approx 4m (4½yds) x 2.5cm (1in) wide ribbon
25mm (1in) diameter large crochet hook

abbreviations
ch chain
dc double crochet
dc2tog Insert hook into next st, draw a loop through, insert hook into next st, draw a loop through, pull through all 3 sts.
st(s) stitch(es)

finished measurement
Length 38cm (15in)
Width at back 33cm (13in)
Width at front 43cm (17in)

tension
Tension is not critical on this project.

method
Make 12ch.
Row 1: 1dc in second ch from hook, 1dc in each ch to end.
Rows 2–5: 1ch (counts as 1dc), 1dc in each st to end. (*12 sts*)
Row 6: 1ch, dc2tog, 1dc in next 8 sts, dc2tog. (*10 sts*)
Rows 7–11: 1ch, 1dc in each st to end. (*10 sts*)
Fasten off.
Weave in ends.

to make up
Cut four pieces of ribbon approx 1m (39in) each length. Attach one piece in each corner of shorter edges.

Egg cosies

Keep your boiled eggs warm with these cute little cosies. Quick to make in the round and using organic yarn, they are perfect gifts or breakfast table treats. Beginners will find these easy and a good way to learn to crochet in the round. Make them with a contrasting border; Improvers can try some beading and bead around the bottom instead.

level 1: Beginner - without beads
level 2: Improver - with beads

materials
Rowan Belle Organic DK (50% organic wool, 50% cotton)
1 x 50g ball (120m/131yds) each of:
012 Tomato
009 Hibiscus
014 Robin's Egg
016 Cilantro
Rooster Almerino DK (50% baby alpaca, 50% merino wool)
1 x 50g ball (112.5m/124yds) 210 Custard
3.5mm (E/4) crochet hook
Sewing needle and thread
6cm (2½in) lengths x 1.5cm (½in) wide ribbon for each cosy
15 x Rowan beads J3001016 (optional)

abbreviations
ch chain
dc double crochet
dc2tog Insert hook into next st, draw a loop through, insert hook into next st, draw a loop through, pull through all 3 sts.
rep repeat
st(s) stitch(es)
ss slip stitch

finished measurement
15.5cm (6in) circumference

tension
Tension is not critical on this project.

method
without beads
Make 2ch, 6dc into second ch from hook.
Round 1: 2dc in each st to end. (*12 sts*)
Round 2: 2dc in each st to end. (*24 sts*)
Rounds 3-7: 1dc in each st.
Round 8: *1dc, dc2tog; rep from * to end. (*16 sts*)
If using a contrasting colour, fasten off here and rejoin new colour into fastened-off st.
Round 9: 1dc in each st, ss into last st.
Fasten off.
Turn cosy right side out.

with beads
Thread 15 beads onto yarn before starting cosy.
Rep Rounds 1-8 of cosy pattern.

Beaded round
Work next round very loosely.
Round 9: Place bead to back of each st and make 1dc in each st, ss into last st.
Fasten off.
Turn cosy with beads on outside.

to make up
Sew in ends.
Cut a piece of ribbon 6cm (2½in) long. Hem the two ends to prevent fraying and sew the ends together to make a tab. Sew onto the top of each cosy.

Cafetière Cosy

A fun and easy project to keep the coffee in your pot toastie and warm. The colours are changed at random as you work, for a multicolour effect.

level 1: Beginner

materials

Rooster Almerino Aran (50% baby alpaca, 50% merino wool)
1 x 50g ball (94m/103yds) each of:
305 Custard
310 Rooster
307 Brighton Rock
309 Ocean
302 Sugared Almond
303 Strawberry Cream
308 Spiced Plum
5mm (H/8) crochet hook
Yarn sewing needle
1 small button

abbreviations

ch chain
dc double crochet
rep repeat
RS right side
ss slip stitch
st(s) stitch(es)
WS wrong side

finished measurement

To fit a medium-size 4–6 cup cafetière, approx 31cm (12in) circumference

tension

16dc x 20 rows over 10cm (4in) square, using 5mm (H/8) hook.

method

Using any colour, make 46ch.
Row 1: 1dc into next ch from hook, 1dc into each ch to end, turn. (*45 sts*)
Row 2: 1ch, 1dc into each st to end.
Rep Row 2, changing colours randomly every 2, 3 or 4 rows, until work measures 16cm (6¼in), or to just above handle of cafetière. Do not fasten off.

Make buttonhole and button tab:
Make 5ch, 1dc into next ch from hook, 1dc into each st to end, turn.
Next row: 1dc into each st to last 4 sts, make 2ch, miss 2 sts, 1dc into each of next 2 sts.
Next row: 1ch, 1dc into each of next 2 sts, 2dc into next ch sp, 1dc into each st to end.
Next row: 1dc into each st to end. Do not fasten off.
Work dc around button tab by making 2dc around side, 1dc in each of the sts underneath to end. Make ss into straight edge.
Fasten off.

to make up

With WS facing, sew a seam 2.5cm (1in) up from the bottom, leaving the remainder open. Turn RS out. Sew a button to correspond with buttonhole. Sew in ends.

method

Using A, make 80ch, join with ss into first ch to make a ring.

Round 1: 2ch, 1htr in each ch, ss into first 2-ch.

Rounds 2–4: 2ch, 1htr in each st, ss into first 2-ch.

Round 5: 1ch, 1dc in each st, join with ss into first ch.

Round 6: 1ch, *1dc in next 18 sts, dc2tog; rep from * to end, join with ss into first ch.

Round 7: Rep Round 5.

Round 8: 2ch, 1htr in each st, ss into first 2-ch.

Round 9: 2ch, *1htr in next 17 sts, htr2tog; rep from * to end, ss into first 2-ch.

Rounds 10–11: Rep Round 8. (68 sts)

Round 12: 1ch, 1dc in next 6 sts, *dc2tog, 1dc in next 6 sts; rep from * to end, ss into first ch. (60 sts)

Rounds 13–14: Rep Round 5.

Round 15: 2ch, *1htr in next 4 sts, htr2tog; rep from * to end, ss into first 2-ch.

Round 16: Rep Round 8.

Round 17: 2ch, *1htr in next 3 sts, htr2tog; rep from * to end, ss into first 2-ch.

Round 18: 2ch, *1htr in next 2 sts, htr2tog; rep from * to last 3 sts, 1htr, htr2tog, ss into first 2-ch.

Round 19: 2ch, *1htr in next st, htr2tog; rep from * to end, ss into first 2-ch.

Round 20: 2ch, *1htr in each st, ss into first 2-ch.

Round 21: 2ch, *htr2tog; rep from * to end, ss into first 2-ch.

Fasten off.

peak

With RS of hat facing, count 21 sts from beg of first round to left. Join yarn in 22nd st, work 1dc into each of next 38 sts, turn.

Rows 1–3: Miss 1 st, 1dc in each st to last 2 sts, miss 1 st, 1dc in last st.

Row 4: Dc2tog twice, 1dc in each st to last 4 sts, dc2tog twice.

Row 5: Miss 1 st, 1dc in each st to last 2 sts, miss 1 st, 1dc in last st.

Row 6: Miss 1 st, dc2tog, 1dc in each st to last 4 sts, dc2tog, miss 1 st, 1dc in last st.

Row 7: Miss 1 st, 1dc in each st to last 2 sts, miss 1 st, 1dc in last st.

Row 8: Rep Row 7 until 14 sts remain.

Fasten off, leaving long strand of yarn for sewing peak.

flower

Using B, make 35ch.

Row 1: 1tr into fifth ch from hook, * 1ch, miss 1ch, (1tr, 1ch, 1tr) in next ch; rep from * to end.

Row 2: 3ch, 5tr in first ch sp, *1dc in next ch sp, 6tr in next ch sp; rep from *, ending with 6tr in last ch sp. (16 shells)

Fasten off, leaving a long tail for sewing flower together.

to make up

To finish peak, thread strand of yarn into yarn sewing needle, turn last two double crochet rows inwards and sew to inside of peak to make a firm edge.

To finish flower, thread needle with yarn tail, weave down side of shell to bottom. Roll first shell tightly to form centre bud. Stitch at base of shell with two stitches to hold in place and roll remaining strip around bud to form rose, securing as you roll by stitching through layers of chains at bottom of rose. Sew rose onto side of hat.

chapter 2

Practice makes perfect

Stripy Wave Cushion

This cushion is a great way to play with colours; I have used bright and cheerful tones in a very soft mix of alpaca and merino wool, but the design would also work well in seaside blues or soft pastels.

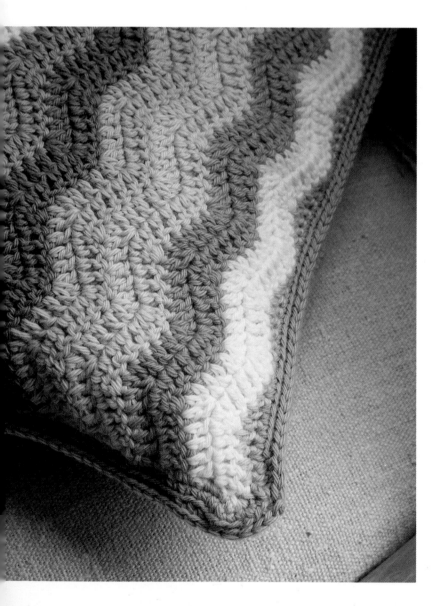

level 2: Improver

materials
Rooster Almerino Aran (50% baby alpaca, 50% merino wool)
1 x 50g ball (94m/103yds) each of:
305 Custard (A)
302 Sugared Almond (B)
307 Brighton Rock (C)
301 Cornish (D)
309 Ocean (E)
303 Strawberry Cream (F)
2 x 50g balls (188m/206yds) 306 Gooseberry (G)
4.5mm (G/6) crochet hook
Yarn sewing needle
40cm (16in) square cushion pad

abbreviations
ch chain
dc double crochet
htr half treble
st(s) stitches
ss slip stitch
tr treble
WS wrong side

special abbreviation
tr3tog Yarn around hook, insert hook into next st, yarn around hook, draw a loop through, yarn around hook and draw through 2 loops on hook (2 loops left on hook). Rep this step into next st (3 loops on hook). Rep this step once more (4 loops on hook), draw yarn through all 4 loops.

finished measurement
To fit a 40cm (16in) square cushion pad

tension
15tr x 8 rows over 10cm (4in) square, using 4.5mm (G/6) hook.

method (make 2 sides)
Using A, make 63ch.

Row 1: 1tr into 2nd ch from hook, 1tr into next ch, * 1tr into each of next 3 ch, tr3tog over next 3 ch, 1tr in next 3-ch, 3tr in next st; rep from * ending last rep with 2tr into last ch, turn.

Row 2: 3ch, 1tr into first st, * 1tr into each of next 3 sts, tr3tog over next 3 sts, 1tr into each of next 3 sts, 3tr in next st; rep from *, ending last rep with 2tr into top of turning chain, turn.
Change to next colour.

*Rep Row 2 twice and change colour; rep from *, changing colour every two rows.
Continue until work measures 37.5cm (15in). Fasten off.

edging
Round 1: With RS facing, join F into fastened-off st.

Side 1:
1ch, 1dc into each of next 2 sts, 1htr in each of next 2 sts, 1tr into next 3 sts, 1htr into next 2 sts, * 1dc into next 3 sts, 1htr into next 2 sts, 1tr into next 3 sts, 1htr into next 2 sts; rep from * to last 2 sts, 1dc in next st, 4dc in corner st.

Side 2:
*Make 4dc into each colour for 6 rows, 5dc evenly in next two rows; rep from * to last two colours, 4dc in each colour. (*63 sts*)

Side 3:
Working on bottom ch from Row 1 of cushion cover, 1tr in next 2 sts, 1htr in next 2 sts; rep from * from side 1 to last 6 sts. 1dc in next 3 sts, 2htr, 1tr, 4dc in corner st.

Side 4:
Repeat side 2, making last 2 sts into corner st. Join with a ss into first ch from side 1. (*63 sts*)

Round 2: 1dc into each st around cushion cover, 4dc in each corner st. Join with a ss into first st. (*252 sts*)

Round 3: Rep Round 2.
Fasten off.

to make up
Sew in ends.

Round 1: Place cushion covers WS together, join G into any st. Make 1dc into each st, 4dc in each corner st, along three sides. Insert cushion pad, continue to make 1dc in each st to end.

Round 2: 1dc into each st around cushion cover, 4dc in each corner st, join with a ss into first st.
Fasten off.
Sew in ends.

tips
Using one of the strong colours for the dc seam will define the outline of the cushion and ties the other colours together.

The increases and decreases should be in line with each other from the previous row – check the alignment as you work. This will ensure that you achieve the 'wave' effect in the pattern.

Baby Blanket

A really beautiful blanket, made with a pretty soft fan stitch and frilled edging – an ideal gift for a newborn.

level 2: Improver

materials

Rooster Baby Rooster (100% fine merino)
8 x 50g balls (1000m/1096yds) 407 Vintage Rose (A)
1 x 50g ball (125m/137yds) 400 Cornish (B)
2 x 50g balls (250m/274yds) 402 Parma Violet (C)
3.5mm (E/4) crochet hook

abbreviations

ch chain
dc double crochet
htr half treble
rep repeat
RS right side
ss slip stitch
st(s) stitch(es)
tr treble

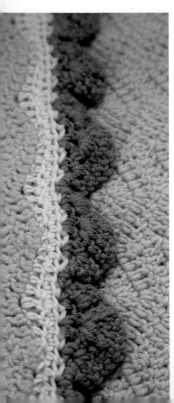

special abbreviation

tr3tog Yarn around hook, insert hook into next st, yarn around hook, draw a loop through, yarn around hook and draw through 2 loops on hook (2 loops left on hook). Rep this step into next st (3 loops on hook). Rep first step once more (4 loops on hook), draw yarn through all 4 loops.

finished measurement

Approx 66 x 89cm (26 x 35in)

tension

Tension is not critical on this project.

method

Using 3.5mm (E/4) hook and A, make 123 ch.
Row 1: 1tr into second ch from hook, 1tr into next ch, * 1tr into each of next 3 ch, tr3tog over next 3 ch, 1tr into each of next 3 ch, 3tr into next ch; rep from *, ending row with 2tr into last ch.
Row 2: 3ch, 1tr into first st, * 1tr into each of next 3 sts, tr3tog over next 3 sts, 1tr into each of next 3 sts, 3tr into next st; rep from * until last 3 sts, 1tr in each st, 2tr into top of turning chain.
Rep Row 2 until work measures approx 87cm (34in).
Fasten off.

edging

Round 1: With RS facing, join col B into fastened-off st.

Side 1:
1ch, 1dc into each of next 2 sts, 1htr, 1tr into next 2 sts, 1htr into next 3 sts, * 1dc into next 3 sts, 1htr into next 2 sts, 1tr into next 3 sts, 1htr into next 2 sts; rep from * to last 2 sts, 1dc in next st, 3dc in corner st. (*125 sts*)

Side 2:
Make 152dc along side to end, make 3dc in corner st. (*155 sts*)

Side 3:
Working on bottom of ch from Row 1 of blanket, 1tr in next 2 sts, 1htr in next 2 sts; rep from * to * from side 1, 1htr, 1tr, 1htr, 1dc in last st. (*125 sts*)

Side 4:
Repeat side 2, making last 2 sts into corner st, join with a ss into first ch from side 1. (*155 sts*)

Round 2: 3ch, 1htr into each st around blanket, 4htr in first 3 corner sts, 5htr into last corner st, join with ss into first st. (*576 sts*)
Fasten off.
Change to C.
Round 3: With RS facing, join yarn into fastened-off st from previous round, * 1ch, miss 1 st, [1dc, 1ch, 1htr] in next st, miss 1 st, [1tr, 1ch, 1tr] in next st, miss 1 st, [1htr, 1ch, 1dc] in next st, 1ch, miss 1 st, ss in next st; rep from * to end, ss last stitch into first ch. Do not fasten off.
Round 4: * 1dc, 1htr in next ch sp, 3tr in next sp (between dc and htr from previous round), [3dtr, 1ch, 3dtr] in next ch sp (between trebles from previous round), 3tr in next sp (between htr and dc from previous round), [1htr, 1dc] in next ch sp, ss in same st as ss from previous row; rep from * to end.
Fasten off.

Chunky Seashell Scarf

Chunky scarves are really popular in all the high street fashion shops, so why not make your own? This project uses beautifully soft chunky wool, has a really contemporary designer look and only takes a couple of evenings to make. What could be better?!

level 2: Improver

materials

Debbie Bliss Como (90% wool, 10% cashmere)
7 x 50g balls (294m/322yds) 06 Duck Egg
7mm (K10½) crochet hook

abbreviations

ch chain
ch sp chain space
dc double crochet
dtr double treble
st(s) stitch(es)
ss slip stitch

finished measurement

Approx 25.5cm (10in) wide x 148cm (58in) long

tension

Tension is not critical on this project.

method

Make 20ch very loosely.
Row 1: Working very loosely on this row, 1dc into second ch from hook and in each of following ch to end.
Row 2: 1dc into first st, *miss 4 sts, 7dtr in next st, 1dc in next st; rep from * to end.
Row 3: 4ch, 1dtr into first dc from previous row, *3ch, miss 3 sts, 1dc in top of next st (top of fan), 3ch, miss 3 sts, 2dtr into top of dc from last row (between shells); rep from *, ending row with 2dtr in last dc of previous row.
Row 4: 1ch, 1dc in next st, *miss next ch sp, make 7dtr into top of dc from previous row, miss 3ch, 1dc in sp between 2dtr from previous row; rep from *, ending row with 1dc in sp between last dtr and turning ch.
Rep Rows 3 and 4 until scarf measures approx 146.5cm (57½in), ending with a Row 4.
Last row: 1ch, *1dc into each 7dtr from previous row, 1ch, 1dc between shells, 1ch; rep from * to end, finishing with 1ch, ss into last st.
Fasten off. Sew in ends.

Floral Curtain Tie-Backs

These curtain ties use very little yarn, so you can use up scraps of any type left over from another project.

level 1: Beginner

materials

Debbie Bliss Cashmerino DK (55% merino wool, 33% microfibre, 12% cashmere)
1 x 50g ball (110m/120yds) 011 Green (A)
Rooster Almerino DK (50% baby alpaca, 50% merino wool)
1 x 50g ball (112.5m/124yds) each of:
211 Brighton Rock (B)
4mm (F/5) crochet hook
Yarn sewing needle

abbreviations

ch chain
dc double crochet
dtr double treble
rep repeat
st(s) stitch(es)
ss slip stitch
tr treble
trtr triple treble

finished measurement

Makes two tie-backs each approx 110cm (43in)

tension

Tension is not critical on this project.

method

Each tie-back has 2 x small roses, 1 x large rose, and 5 petal flowers.

petal flower (make 10)

Using A, make 6ch, join with ss into first ch.
Make 16dc into circle, joining tail into each dc around circle, join with a ss. Change to B.

*3ch, 1tr into next 2 sts, 3ch, ss into next st; rep from * 4 more times.
(*5 petals*)
Fasten off.
Pull tail to close up centre hole and sew in ends.

small roses (make 4)

Make 48ch.
Petals 1–3: Miss 3ch, 1tr in each of next 2ch, 2ch, ss in next ch, *3ch, 1tr in each of next 2 ch, 2ch, ss in next ch; rep from * to end once more. (*3 petals*)
Petals 4–6: *4ch, 1dtr in each of next 4 ch, 3ch, ss in next ch; rep from * twice more.
Petals 7–9: *4ch, 1dtr in each of next 6 ch, 3ch, ss in next ch; rep from * twice more.
Fasten off.

Large roses (make 2)

Make 99ch.
Petals 1–4: Miss 3ch, 1tr in each of next 2 ch, 2ch, ss in next ch, [3ch, 1tr in each of next 2 ch, 2ch, ss in next ch] 3 times.
Petals 5–8: [4ch, 1dtr in each of next 4 ch, 3ch, ss in next ch] 4 times.
Petals 9–12: [4ch, 1dtr in each of next 6 ch, 3ch, ss in next ch] 4 times.
Petals 13–16: [5ch, 1trtr in each of next 8ch, 4ch, ss in next ch] 4 times.
Fasten off.

to make up

To make roses, press petals flat. Starting with smaller petals, coil petals, keeping base flat at chain edge, and stitch in place as you go.

Make two lengths of chains for each tie-back, each 54cm (21in) long. Fasten off. Attach one end of one chain to back of one small rose, leave 10cm (4in) gap then attach chain to back of large rose. Make 2.5cm (1in) loop at other end of chain and secure in place. Attach one end of other chain to back of other small rose, leave 7.5cm (3in) gap and attach chain to back of large rose. Cross second chain over top of first chain and attach in place, so chains are secured and crossed at back. Place five petal flowers evenly along chain, attach to chain leaving 2.5cm (1in) gap between each one and allowing enough space at other end for 2.5cm (1in) loop as first chain. Rep for second tie-back.

Felted Beaded Bracelet

This very pretty bracelet must be made using 100% pure wool, so that it will felt correctly. It's felted by washing it in the washing machine before sewing on the beads.

level 2: Improver

materials

Cascade 220 DK (100% Peruvian wool)
1 x 100g hank (200m/220yds) 7802 Bright Pink
4mm (F/5) crochet hook
2cm (1in) wide ribbon x wrist measurement plus 1.5cm (½in) at each end for hem
2cm (1in) wide pink felt x wrist measurement
Sewing needle and thread
9 seed beads
1 small press stud

abbreviations

ch chain
dc double crochet
st(s) stitch(es)
ss slip stitch
tr treble
WS wrong side

finished measurement

2cm (1in) wide x wrist circumference

tension

Tension is not critical on this project.

method

flowers (make 3)

Make 5ch, join with a ss to make a ring.
Round 1: *1dc, 1tr, 1dc into ring; rep from * 3 more times. (4 petals)
Round 2: *2ch, from WS ss into base of second dc of next petal (pick up 2 loops); rep from * 3 more times, slip last st into joining st. (4 loops)
Round 3: *4tr into next 2-ch sp at back, ss into same ch sp; rep from * 3 more times.
Fasten off.

to make up

Place flowers in the washing machine on a 60ºC wash. Allow to dry naturally.

Sew three beads into centre of each flower. Sew flowers in a group on centre of ribbon. Hem each end of ribbon. Sew felt to back of ribbon. Sew press stud in place.

Fingerless Gloves

These delicate fingerless gloves are charming and are also a good project to try out some edging skills.

level 2: Improver

materials

Debbie Bliss Cashmerino DK (55% merino wool, 33% microfibre, 12% cashmere)
2 x 50g balls (220m/240yds) 022 Raspberry Pink
3.75mm (E/4) crochet hook

abbreviations

ch chain
dc double crochet
inc including
rep repeat
st(s) stitch(es)
ss slip stitch
tr treble

finished measurement

To fit an average size woman's hand

tension

Tension is not critical on this project.

method

glove (make 2)

Make 36ch, join with ss into first ch to make a ring.

Round 1: 1ch, miss 1 ch, 1dc in each of next 35ch, join with a ss into next ch. (35 sts)

Round 2: 6ch, miss 3 sts, 1tr, *3ch, miss 3 sts, 1tr; rep from * six times, 3ch, ss into third of first 6ch. (9 spaces)

Round 3: 1ch, miss 1 st, 1dc in each of next 35 sts, join with a ss into next st. (35 sts)

Rounds 4-9: Rep Round 3. (35 sts)

Round 10: 1ch, *miss 1 st, 1dc in each of next 4 sts; rep from * to last 2 sts, 1dc in next st, join with a ss into next st. (29 sts)

Round 11: 1ch, miss 1 st, *1dc in each of next 29 sts, join with a ss into next st. (29 sts)

Round 12: 1ch, miss 1 st, *1dc in each of next 3 sts, 2dc in next st; rep from * to last st, join with a ss into next st. (36 sts)

Rounds 13-21: Rep Round 3. (36 sts)

Round 22 (left glove only): 1ch, miss 1 st, 1dc in each of next 2 sts, 5ch, miss 5 sts, 1dc in next st, 1dc in each st to last st, join with a ss into next st.

Round 22 (right glove only): 1ch, miss 1 st, 1dc in each st to last 7 sts, 5ch, miss 5 sts, 1dc in next 2 sts, join with a ss into next st.

Round 23: 1ch, miss 1 st, 1dc in each st (including into each 5ch from previous round), join with a ss into next st. (36 sts)

Rounds 24-26: 1ch, miss 1 st, 1dc into next 36 sts, join with a ss into next st. (36 sts)

Round 27: 1ch, *miss next st, 1dc in each of next 8 sts; rep from * twice more, miss next st, 1dc in each st to last st, join with a ss into next st. (33 sts)

Rounds 28-30: Rep Round 3. (33 sts)

Round 31: *5ch, miss 3 sts, 1dc into next st; rep from * 7 times more, 3ch, 1tr into base of first 5-ch.

Round 32: *5ch, 1dc into 3rd of 5ch from previous round; rep from * 7 times more, 3ch, 1tr into top of tr from previous round.

Round 33: Rep Round 32 to last dc, 5ch, ss into top of first 5-ch from previous round.
Fasten off.

thumb

Rejoin yarn to thumbhole created by Rounds 22-23.

Round 1: 1ch, 1dc into each of 5 sts at top of hole, make 1dc in each of 5 sts at bottom of thumbhole, join with a ss into first ch.

Round 2: 1ch, miss 1 st, 1dc in next 9 sts, join with a ss into next st.

Rounds 3-5: Rep Round 2.
Fasten off.

edging

Join yarn into start st at wrist end of glove.

Round 1: *5ch, miss 5 sts, 1dc into next st; rep from * to end.

Round 2: *5tr into first ch sp, ss into next dc from previous round; rep from * to end. Ss into base of first 5tr.
Fasten off.
Sew in ends.

---

tip
To achieve a straight seam with this project, take care when counting stitches in each round.

Swishy Scarf

This scarf is made with half trebles in the middle and is crocheted horizontally, with a lacy edging. If you are a beginner, make 4-5 more rows of half trebles than in the pattern, if you are an intermediate crochet worker, have a go at the pretty edging.

level 2: Improver

materials

Rooster Almerino DK (50% baby alpaca, 50% merino wool)
3 x 50g balls (337.5m/372yds) 201 Cornish
4mm (F/5) crochet hook

abbreviations

ch chain
ch sp chain space
dc double crochet
dtr double treble
htr half treble
st(s) stitch(es)
ss slip stitch
tr treble

finished measurement

Approx 157 x 11cm (62 x 4½in)

tension

Tension is not critical on this project.

method

Make 258ch.
Row 1: 1htr in second ch from hook, 1htr in each ch to end.
Rows 2-3: 2ch, 1htr in each st to end. Do not fasten off.

Edging:
Work in rounds, not in rows. Do not turn at end of round.
Round 1: *3ch, miss 3 sts, 1dc into next st**; rep from * to ** until first corner, 3ch, 1dc into middle of second row of side edge, 3ch, 1dc into next corner; rep from * to ** to next corner, 3ch, 1dc into middle of second row of side edge, 3ch, join with ss into base of first 3-ch.
Round 2: 2tr, 3ch, 2tr into middle st of first 3-ch from previous round. *2tr, 3ch, 2tr into middle st of next 3-ch from previous round; rep from * to end of round, join with ss into top of first 2-tr.
Round 3: Ss into middle st of first 3ch from previous round, *5ch, ss into middle st of next 3-ch from previous round; rep from * to end, 5ch, ss into first ss.
Round 4: *5dc into 5ch sp; rep from * to end, join with ss into ss from previous round.
Round 5: *1dc into first st, 1ch, 1htr, 1ch, 1tr into next st, [1ch, 1dtr, 1ch] 3 times into next st, 1tr, 1ch, 1htr into next st, 1ch, 1dc into next st, ss into ss from previous round; rep from * to end, join with a ss into ss from previous round. Fasten off.
Sew in ends.

Baby Bouncers

Little crochet balls for tiny hands – lovely for babies to hold, throw or crawl after. These are great to practice crocheting in the round. Make them using one colour or with stripes.

level 1: Beginner

materials
Small amounts of each of:
King Cole Merino Blend DK (100% merino wool)
55 Gold
787 Fuchsia

Debbie Bliss Cashmerino DK (55% merino wool, 33% microfibre, 12% cashmere)
017 Lilac
029 Light Green
Rowan Belle Organic DK (50% organic wool, 50% cotton)
014 Robin's Egg
Rooster Almerino DK (50% baby alpaca, 50% merino wool)
203 Strawberry Cream

4mm (F/5) crochet hook
Fibrefill stuffing

abbreviations
beg beginning
ch chain
dc double crochet
dc2tog Insert hook into next st, draw a loop through, insert hook into next st, draw a loop through, pull through all 3 sts.
st(s) stitch(es)
ss slip stitch

finished measurement
7.5cm (3in) diameter

tension
Tension is not critical on this project.

method
Place st marker at beg of each round.
Round 1: 2ch, 6dc into second ch from hook.
Round 2: 2dc in each st. (*12 sts*)
Round 3: *1dc in next st, 2dc; rep from * to end. (*18 sts*)
Round 4: *1dc in next 2 sts, 2dc; rep from * to end. (*24 sts*)
Round 5: *1dc in next 3 sts, 2dc; rep from * to end. (*30 sts*)
Rounds 6–10: 1dc in each st. (*30 sts*)
Round 11: *1dc in next 3 sts, dc2tog; rep from * to end. (*24 sts*)
Round 12: *1dc in next 2 sts, dc2tog; rep from * to end. (*18 sts*)
Round 13: *1dc in next st, dc2tog; rep from * to end. (*12 sts*)
Stuff ball.
Round 14: Dc2tog around until hole closes.
Fasten off.
Sew in ends.

Chunky Luscious Cushion

This gorgeous cushion is made using a hand-dyed chunky wool in beautiful soft tones. It uses a fairly large hook and thick yarn, so takes no time at all to make.

level 2: Improver

materials
Fyberspates Scrumptious Chunky (45% silk, 55% wool)
5 x 100g hanks (610m/667yds) Copper Spring
6mm (J/10) crochet hook
Yarn sewing needle
3 x 4cm (1½in) buttons
45.5cm (18in) square cushion pad

abbreviations
ch chain
dc double crochet
rep repeat
st(s) stitch(es)
ss slip stitch
tr treble

special abbreviation
tr2tog Yarn around hook, insert hook into next st, yarn around hook, draw a loop through, yarn around hook and draw through 2 loops on hook (2 loops left on hook). Rep this step into next st (3 loops on hook), draw yarn through all 3 loops.

finished measurement
To fit a 45.5cm (18in) square cushion pad

tension
13tr x 7 rows over 4in (10cm) square using 6mm (J/10) hook.

method
Make 51ch.
Row 1: 1tr in fourth ch from hook, 1tr in next ch (tr2tog over next 2ch) twice, 1tr in next ch, 2tr in next ch, *2tr in next ch, 1tr in next ch, (tr2tog over next 2ch) twice, 1tr in next ch, 2tr in next ch; rep from * to end.
Row 2: 3ch, 1tr in first tr, 1tr in next tr, (tr2tog over next 2 sts) twice, 1tr in next tr, 2tr in next tr, *2tr in next tr, 1tr in next tr, (tr2tog over next 2 sts) twice, 1tr in next tr, 2tr in next tr; rep from * to first 3ch, work last 2tr into third of first 3ch.
Rep Row 2 until work measures 99cm (39in).
Next row: 3ch, 1tr in first tr, 1tr in next tr, (tr2tog over next 2 sts) twice, 1tr in next tr, *4ch, miss 2 sts, 1tr in next tr, (tr2tog over next 2 sts) twice, 1tr in next tr, 2tr in each of next 2tr, 1tr in next tr, (tr2tog over next 2 sts) twice, 1tr in next tr*; rep from * to*, 4ch, miss next 2 sts, 1tr in next tr, (tr2tog over next 2 sts) twice, 1tr in next tr, 2tr in next tr, turn.
Work 2 more rows as Row 2, working into each of 4-ch as if a tr.

to make up
With RS facing, fold from bottom to 10cm (4in) from top. Fold top flap so it overlaps bottom. Ensure cushion cover measures 45.5cm (18in). Dc side seams together. Sew on buttons to correspond with buttonholes.

Baby Bibs

These cute, pretty bibs are made using a 100% cotton yarn, so it's easy to wash off mucky mealtime mayhem.

level 2: Improver

materials
Colourway 1
Rowan Handknit Cotton DK (100% cotton)
1 x 50g ball (85m/93yds) each of:
303 Sugar (A)
251 Ecru (B)
Debbie Bliss Cotton DK (100% cotton)
1 x 50g ball (84m/92yds) 49 Mauve (C)

Colourway 2
Debbie Bliss Cotton DK (100% cotton)
1 x 50g ball (84m/92yds) each of:
51 Sky (A)

09 Duck Egg Blue (C)
Rowan Handknit Cotton DK (100% cotton)
1 x 50g ball (85m/93yds) 251 Ecru (B)

3mm (D/3) and 4mm (F/5) crochet hooks

abbreviations
ch chain
dc double crochet
dc2tog Insert hook into next st, draw a loop through, insert hook into next st, draw a loop through, pull through all 3 sts.
st(s) stitch(es)
ss slip stitch

finished measurement
Approx 13 x 19cm (5¼ x 7½in)

tension
Tension is not critical on this project.

method

Using 4mm (F/5) hook and A, make 21ch.

Row 1: 1dc into next ch from hook, 1dc in each ch to end. *(20 sts)*
Row 2: 1ch, 1dc in each st to end. *(20 sts)*
Rows 3–5: 1ch, 2dc in first st, 1dc in each st to last st, 2dc. *(26 sts)*
Change to B.
Row 6: 1dc in each st to end. *(26 sts)*
Row 7: 1ch, 1dc in each st to end.
Change to A.
Row 8: 1dc in each st to end.
Change to B.
Rows 9–10: 1dc in each st to end.
Change to A.
Rows 11–15: 1dc in each st to end.
Change to B.
Rows 16–17: 1dc in each st to end.
Change to A.
Row 18: 1dc in each st to end.
Rows 19–20: 1ch, 1dc in each st to end.

Neck edge
Row 21: 1ch, 1dc in each of next 7 sts, turn. *(7 sts)*
Row 22: 1ch, dc2tog, 1dc in each of next 3 sts, dc2tog. *(5 sts)*
Row 23: 1ch, dc2tog, 1dc in next st, dc2tog. *(3 sts)*
Rows 24–25: 1ch, 1dc in each st. *(3 sts)*
Row 26: 1ch, miss 1 st, 1dc.
Row 27: 1ch, dc2tog.
Fasten off.
Join A to other edge of bib.
Row 1: 1ch, 1dc in each of next 7 sts. *(7 sts)*
Rows 2–7: Same as Rows 22–27
Fasten off.

Edging

Bottom edge
Turn bib upside down and start edging by working from bottom. Using 4mm (F/5) hook and C, join yarn in bottom right-hand corner, make 18dc.

Side edge 1
Miss one sp, make ss into next space, 26dc up side edging to tip. Do not fasten off.

Tie 1
35ch, 1dc in second ch from hook, 1dc in next 33 ch.

Neck edge
8dc along first curve, 13dc along straight edge, 8dc along second curve. Do not fasten off.

Tie 2
35ch, 1dc in second ch from hook, 1dc in next 33 ch.

Side edge
26dc down side edging. Miss last space and make ss into first dc from bottom edge. Do not fasten off.

Using 3mm (D/3) hook, make 1dc into each st around side, ties and neck edgings, join with a ss into first dc.

Baby Slippers

I originally saw a pattern for similar slippers in a vintage magazine, but they were made in hard cotton. I've adapted it for lovely soft 100% wool and made these cute slippers a little deeper with a pretty picot edging.

level 2: Improver

materials
Colourway 1
Rooster Baby Rooster (100% fine merino)
1 x 50g ball (125m/137yds) each of:
409 Pistachio (A)
400 Cornish (B)
402 Parma Violet (C)

Colourway 2
Rooster Baby Rooster (100% fine merino)
1 x 50g ball (125m/137yds) each of:
409 Pistachio (A)
405 Ice Gem (B)
400 Cornish (C)

3mm (D/3) crochet hook

abbreviations
ch chain
dc double crochet
htr half treble
st(s) stitch(es)
ss slip stitch
tr treble

finished measurement
To fit a baby 0–3 months old

tension
Tension is not critical on this project.

method
sole (make two)
Using A, make 11ch.
Round 1: 1htr in third ch from hook, 1htr in next 7 sts, 6htr in last ch. Working on opposite side of ch, 1htr in next 7 ch, 5htr in last ch, join with a ss in top first htr. (26 sts)
Round 2: 1ch, 1htr in next 8 sts, 2htr in each of next 5 ch, htr in next 8 sts, 2htr in each of next 5 sts, join with a ss in top of first htr. (36 sts)
Round 3: 1ch, 1htr in next 8 sts, [2htr in first st, 1htr in next st] 5 times, 1htr in next 8 sts [2htr in first st, 1htr] 5 times, join with a ss in top of first htr. (46 sts)

Upper slipper
Round 1: 1ch. Working in back loop of sts only. 1dc in each st to end, join

with a ss into first dc (46 sts). (This forms ridge on outside of sole.)

Round 2: 3ch, 1tr in same st, *miss 2 sts, 3tr in next st; rep from * 14 more times, 1tr in same st as ss of previous round, join with a ss in top of first 3ch. (46 sts – 16 groups of tr)

Fasten off.

Using B, join in at top of fastened off st.

Round 3: 3ch, 1tr in same st, miss 2 sts, 3tr in next st (top of first group of tr), miss next 2 sts, 3tr in next st, *miss next 2 sts, 1tr in next st; rep from * 5 more times, **miss 2 sts, 3tr in next st; rep from ** 5 more times, 1tr in same st as ss of previous round, join with a ss in top of first 3ch.

Fasten off.

Front

Using B and working at toe end with toe facing, join yarn to top of second single tr on right of work.

Row 1: 1ch, 1dc in same st, 1dc in next 3 sts, miss next st, ss in next 2 sts, turn.

Row 2: Miss 2 ss from previous row, 1dc in next 4 sts, miss next st, ss in next 2 sts, turn.

Row 3: Miss 2 ss from previous row, 1dc in each of next 4 sts, ss in next 2 sts, turn.

Row 4: Miss 2 ss from previous row, 1dc in each of next 4 sts, ss in next 2 sts, turn.

Row 5: 1ch, 1dc in each st around bootie, join with a ss in first dc. (32 sts)

Fasten off.

Row 6: Join in C to fastened-off st, *3ch, ss into bottom of 3ch, miss 1 st; ss into next st, rep from * to end.

Fasten off.

Sew in ends.

chapter 3

Confident crocheting

Camellia Blanket

This is a light, beautiful blanket that will brighten your room at any time of year, but the colours evoke the delicate pinks and pale silver colours of summer.

level 3: Enthusiast

materials
Inner Flowers:
Debbie Bliss Cashmerino Aran (55% merino wool, 33% microfibre, 12% cashmere)
3 x 50g balls (270m/294yds) each of:
019 Lilac (A)
026 Pink (B)
Debbie Bliss Cashmerino DK (55% merino wool, 33% microfibre, 12% cashmere)
3 x 50g balls (330m/360yds) 023 Peach (C)

Leaf:
Debbie Bliss Cashmerino DK (55% merino wool, 33% microfibre, 12% cashmere)
5 x 50g balls (550m/600yds) 011 Green (D)

One-colour squares:
Debbie Bliss Cashmerino Aran (55% merino wool, 33% microfibre, 12% cashmere)
32 x 50g balls (2880m/3136yds) 027 Silver Grey (MC)

4.5mm (G/6) crochet hook

abbreviations
ch chain
ch sp chain space
dc double crochet
ss slip stitch
st(s) stitch(es)
tr treble
WS wrong side

finished measurement
Approx 170 x 125cm (67 x 49in)

tension
Tension is not critical on this project.

method

The blanket is made up of a combination of flower squares and single-colour squares. Make a total of 143 squares: 25 x A centre flower, 24 x B centre flower, 23 x C centre flower (72 flower squares) and 71 single colour squares.

flower square

Using A, B or C, 5ch, join with a ss

Round 1: *1dc, 1tr, 1dc into ring; rep from * 3 more times. (*4 petals*)

Round 2: *2ch, from WS ss into base of 2nd dc of next petal (pick up 2 loops); rep from * 3 more times. Slip last stitch into first ss. (*4 loops*)

Round 3: *4tr into next 2ch sp (at back), ss into same ch sp; rep from * 3 more times.

Fasten off.

Continue working with same colour. Work into the back of petals, picking up two loops.

Join yarn at base of highest point of previous round.

Round 4: *3ch, ss into middle of base of the next petal; rep from * 3 more times. Slip last st into joining st.

Round 5: *8tr into next 3ch sp, ss into same 3ch sp; rep from * 3 more times. Slip last st into joining st.

Fasten off.

Change to D. Working into back of petals and picking up two loops as follows, join yarn into middle of base of petal (next 8tr) of previous round.

Round 6: *3ch, ss into middle of base of the next petal; rep from * 3 more times. Slip last st into joining st.

Round 7: *10tr into 3ch sp, ss into same 3ch sp; rep from * 3 more times.

Fasten off.

Change to MC.

Working into stitches at top (not at back), join yarn into top of centre tr of one leaf.

Round 8: 4ch (counts as 1tr, 1ch), *3tr into next space between leaves, 1ch, 3tr, 2ch, 3tr into top of 5th tr of next leaf, 1ch; rep from * twice more. 3tr, 1ch into space between next leaves, 1ch, 3tr, 2ch, 2tr into same st as start of round, ss into ch sp made from first 4-ch.

Round 9: 3ch, 2tr into same ch sp, 1ch, 3tr into next ch sp, *1ch, 3tr, 2ch, 3tr into next ch sp, 1ch, 3tr into next ch sp, 1ch, 3tr into next ch sp; rep from * twice more. 1ch, 3tr, 2ch, 3tr into next ch sp, 1ch, ss into top of first 3-ch.

Round 10: 1ch, 1dc in top of next 3 sts, 1dc in next ch sp, 1dc in top of next 3 sts, 1dc in next ch sp, *1dc in top of next 3 sts, 2dc in next ch sp, 1dc in top of next 3 sts, 1dc in next ch sp, 1dc in top of next 3 sts, 1dc in next ch sp, 1dc in top of next 3 sts, 1dc in next ch sp; rep from * twice more. 1dc in top of next 3 sts, 2dc in next ch sp, 1dc in top of next 3 sts, 1dc in next ch sp, ss into first ch.

Fasten off.

One-colour squares

Using MC, make 4ch, join with a ss.

Round 1: 5ch (counts as 1tr and 2ch), *3tr into ring, 2ch; rep from * twice more, 2tr, ss into 3rd of 5-ch.

Round 2: Ss into next ch sp, 5ch (counts as 1tr and 2ch), 3tr into same sp, *1ch, [3tr, 2ch, 3tr] into next chain sp; rep from * twice more, 1ch, miss 3 sts, 2tr into same space as 5ch from previous round, ss into 3rd of 5-ch.

Round 3: Ss into next ch sp, 5ch (counts as 1tr and 2ch), 3tr into same sp, *1ch, miss 3tr, 3tr into next ch sp, 1ch, miss 3tr**, [3tr, 2ch, 3tr] into next sp; rep from * twice more and then from * to ** once more, 2tr into same space as 5ch, ss into 3rd of 5-ch.

Round 4: Ss into next ch sp, 5ch (counts as 1tr and 2ch), 3tr into same sp, *[1ch, miss 3tr; 3tr into next ch sp] twice, 1ch, miss 3tr**, [3tr, 2ch, 3tr] into next ch sp; rep from * twice more and from * to ** once more, 2tr into same space as 5ch, ss into 3rd of 5-ch.

Round 5: 1ch, 1dc into top of next st, 2dc into next ch sp, 1dc into top of next 3 sts, 1dc into next ch sp, 1dc into top of next 3 sts, 1dc into next ch sp, 1dc into top of next 3 sts, 1dc into next ch sp, 1dc into top of next 3 sts, *2dc into next ch sp, 1dc into top of next 3 sts, 1dc into next ch sp, 1dc into top of next 3 sts, 1dc into next ch sp, 1dc into top of next 3 sts, 1dc into next ch sp, 1dc into top of next 3 sts; rep from * once more. 2dc into next ch sp, 1dc into top of next 3 sts, 1dc into next ch sp, 1dc into top of next 3 sts, 1dc into next ch sp, 1dc into top of next 3 sts, 1dc into next ch sp, 1dc into top of next 2 sts, ss into top of first ch.

Fasten off.

to make up

The blanket is 11 squares wide x 13 squares long, with alternating flower squares and one-colour squares. Place different-coloured flowers at random over the blanket and then join the squares using a dc seam. Make edging around edge of blanket by making 1dc into each st along each edge, making 5dc into each of 4 corner stitches. Fasten off. Sew in ends.

tips

The flower centres are mostly in Aran weight, but I've also chosen a peach and green that only come in DK. This makes no difference to the size and shape of the blanket, so if you choose your own palette any similar mix of DK and Aran wool will work just as well. However, if you choose to make the blanket using only DK wool, the measurements will come up smaller.

Sew in ends after completing each square to avoid having to do them all at the end.

Next row: 1ch, 1dc in each st to end.
Next row: 1ch, dc2tog, 1dc in each st to last 2 sts, dc2tog. (20 sts)
Next row: 1ch, 1dc in each st to end.
Next row: 1ch, 1dc in each st to end.
Next row: 1ch, dc2tog, 1dc in each st to last 2 sts, dc2tog. (18 sts)
Next row: 1ch, dc2tog, 1dc in each st to last 2 sts, dc2tog. (16 sts)
Next row: 1ch, dc2tog, 1dc in each st to last 2 sts, dc2tog. (14 sts)
Next row: 1ch, dc2tog, 1dc in each st to last 2 sts, dc2tog. (12 sts)
Next row: 1ch, dc2tog, 1dc in each st to last 2 sts, dc2tog. (10 sts)
Next row: 1ch, dc2tog, 1dc in each st to last 2 sts, dc2tog. (8 sts)
Next row: 1ch, 1dc in each st to end.
Fasten off.

top tab
Using one strand of B and 4mm (F/5) hook, make 5ch, 1dc into second
ch from hook, 1dc in each of next 3 ch to end, 1ch, turn. (4 sts)
Next row: 1dc in each st to end, 1ch, turn. (4 sts)
Continue until work measures approx 15cm (6in).
Fasten off.

roses
Make approx 29 roses in a variety of different colours – enough to cover
each side on the top half of the cosy.
Using 4mm (F/5) or 3.5mm (E/4) hook and a scrap of yarn, make 48ch.
Petals 1–3: Miss 3 ch, 1tr in each of next 2 ch, 2ch, ss in next ch, *3ch,
1tr in each of next 2 ch, 2ch, ss in next ch; rep from * once more. (3 petals)
Petals 4–6: *4ch, 1dtr in each of next 4 ch, 3ch, ss in next ch; rep from
* twice more.
Petals 7–9: *4ch, 1dtr in each of next 6 ch, 3ch, ss in next ch; rep from
* twice more.
Fasten off.

to make up
With WS facing, pin tea cosy sides together, leaving a gap on each side
for handle and spout; try it on the tea pot and pin to fit, or pin and sew
2.5cm (1in) at bottom of each side, leaving a 10cm (4in) gap on each
side. Fold tab in half and pin in place to top centre of cosy. Sew seams
across the top and down sides.

embroidery and roses
Using C, embroider leaves in chain stitch along the top edge of cream
section on both sides.

Press rose petals flat. Starting with smaller petals, coil petals, keeping the
base flat at chain edge and stitching in place as you go. Sew roses tightly
together on each side at the top of cosy.

tip
Crocheting using the yarn doubled up
makes the fabric thicker and so better
for insulating.

Russian Dolls – Babushkas

These dolls are such fun to make and look really cute decorated with embroidered flowers or little crochet flowers. The stitches are very easy, but because the dolls are small, they can be fiddly and require attention to detail, so I have put them at Enthusiast level – but don't let that put you off.

level 3: Enthusiast

materials

Large doll
Rooster Almerino DK (50% baby alpaca, 50% merino wool)
1 x 50g ball (112.5m/124yds) each of:
214 Damson (A)
201 Cornish (B)
213 Cherry (C)
Debbie Bliss Baby Cashmerino (55% merino wool, 33% microfibre, 12% cashmere)
1 x 50g ball (125m/137yds) 011 Chocolate Brown for eyes and hair
Red embroidery thread for mouth

Medium doll
Rowan Pure Wool DK (100% superwash wool)
1 x 50g ball (125m/137yds) 036 Kiss (D)
Rooster Almerino DK (50% baby alpaca, 50% merino wool)
1 x 50g ball (112.5m/124yds) each of:
201 Cornish (E)
207 Gooseberry (F)
210 Custard for hair
Rowan Cashsoft 4 ply (58% extra-fine merino, 33% microfibre, 10% cashmere)
1 x 50g ball (180m/197yds) 433 Cream (G)
Black embroidery thread for eyes
Red embroidery thread for mouth

Small doll
Rooster Almerino DK (50% baby alpaca, 50% merino wool)
1 x 50g ball (112.5m/124yds) each of:
211 Brighton Rock (H)
201 Cornish (I)
208 Ocean (J)
201 Custard for hair

Rowan Cashsoft 4 ply (58% extra-fine merino, 33% microfibre, 10% cashmere)
1 x 50g ball (180m/197yds) 433 Cream (K)
Black embroidery thread for eyes
Red embroidery thread for mouth

Tiny doll
Debbie Bliss Rialto DK (100% extra fine merino wool)
1 x 50g ball (105m/114.5yds) 10 Green (L)
Rooster Almerino DK (50% baby alpaca, 50% merino wool)
1 x 50g ball (112.5m/124yds) 201 Cornish (M)
Rowan Pure Wool DK (100% superwash wool)
1 x 50g ball (125m/137yds) 036 Kiss (N)
Debbie Bliss Baby Cashmerino (55% merino wool, 33% microfibre, 12% cashmere)
1 x 50g ball (125m/137yds) 011 Chocolate Brown for hair
Rowan Cashsoft 4 ply (58% extra-fine merino, 33% microfibre, 10% cashmere)
1 x 50g ball (180m/197yds) 433 Cream (O)
Black embroidery thread for eyes
Red embroidery thread for mouth

Babushka flowers
Small amount of yarn in each of:
Rooster Almerino DK (50% baby alpaca, 50% merino wool)
211 Brighton Rock
210 Custard
207 Gooseberry
203 Strawberry Cream
213 Cherry
Rowan Pure Wool DK (100% superwash wool)
036 Kiss

Leaves
Small amount of yarn in:
Debbie Bliss Rialto DK (100% extra-fine merino wool)
10 Green
Rooster Almerino DK (50% baby alpaca, 50% merino wool)
207 Gooseberry

Fibrefill stuffing
4mm (F/5), 3.5mm (E/4) and 3mm (D/3) crochet hooks
Yarn sewing needle

abbreviations
beg beginning
ch chain
cont continue
dc double crochet
dc2tog Insert hook into next st, draw a loop through, insert hook into next st, draw a loop through, pull through all 3 sts.
rep repeat
st(s) stitch(es)

special abbreviation
Reverse dc (crab st) Do not turn at end of row. Instead, working from left to right, insert hook in next st to right, yarn around hook, draw yarn through st, yarn around hook, draw yarn through 2 loops on hook.

finished measurements
Large 22cm (9in) high
Medium 15cm (6in) high
Small 11cm (4½ in) high
Tiny 9cm (3½in) high

tension
Tension is not critical on this project.

method
Place st marker at beg of each round.

large doll body
Using 4mm (F/5) hook and A, make 2ch.
Round 1: 6dc into second ch from hook. (6 *sts*)
Round 2: 2dc in each st. (12 *sts*)
Round 3: *1dc in next st, 2dc in next st; rep from * to end. (18 *sts*)
Round 4: *1dc in each of next 2 sts, 2dc in next st; rep from * to end. (24 *sts*)
Round 5: *1dc in each of next 3 sts, 2dc in next st; rep from * to end. (30 *sts*)
Round 6: *1dc in each of next 4 sts, 2dc in next st; rep from * to end. (36 *sts*)
Round 7: *1dc in each of next 5 sts, 2dc in next st; rep from * to end. (42 *sts*)
Round 8: *1dc in each of next 6 sts, 2dc in next st; rep from * to end. (48 *sts*)
Rounds 9–13: 1dc in each st. (48 *sts*)
Change to B.
Round 14: Dc2tog, 1dc in each of next 22 sts, dc2tog, 1dc in each of next 22 sts. (46 *sts*)
Round 15: 1dc in each st.

Round 16: Dc2tog, 1dc in each of next 21 sts, dc2tog, 1dc in each of next 21 sts. (44 *sts*)
Round 17: Dc2tog, 1dc in each of next 20 sts, dc2tog, 1dc in each of next 20 sts. (42 *sts*)
Round 18: 1dc in each st.
Round 19: Dc2tog, 1dc in each of next 19 sts, dc2tog, 1dc in each of next 19 sts. (40 *sts*)
Round 20: 1dc in each st.
Round 21: Dc2tog, 1dc in each of next 18 sts, dc2tog, 1dc in each of next 18 sts. (38 *sts*)
Round 22: Dc2tog, 1dc in each of next 17 sts, dc2tog, 1dc in each of next 17 sts. (36 *sts*)
Round 23: 1dc in each st.
Round 24: Dc2tog, 1dc in each of next 16 sts, dc2tog, 1dc in each of next 16 sts. (34 *sts*)
Round 25: 1dc in each st. (30 *sts*)

Round 26: Dc2tog, 1dc in each of next 15 sts, dc2tog, 1dc in each of next 15 sts. (32 sts)

Round 27: Dc2tog, 1dc in each of next 14 sts, dc2tog, 1dc in each of next 14 sts. (30 sts)

Round 28: 1dc in each st.

Round 29: Dc2tog, 1dc in each of next 13 sts, dc2tog, 1dc in each of next 13 sts. (28 sts)

Change to C. Work next round in reverse dc.

Round 30: 1 reverse dc, *make 5ch, 1dc (standard) in second ch from hook, 1dc (standard) in next 4 ch, ss in next st; rep from * once more (headscarf ties). Cont in reverse dc to end. (28 sts)

Stop working in reverse dc and cont in standard dc.

Round 31: 1dc into back of each st in B from Round 29 to end. (28 sts)

Round 32: Dc2tog, 1dc in each of next 12 sts, dc2tog, 1dc in each of next 12 sts. (26 sts)

Rounds 33–34: 1dc in each st. (26 sts)

Round 35: Dc2tog, 1dc in each of next 11 sts, dc2tog, 1dc in each of next 11 sts. (24 sts)

Round 36: Dc2tog, 1dc in each of next 10 sts, dc2tog, 1dc in each of next 10 sts. (22 sts)

Round 37: Dc2tog, 1dc in each of next 9 sts, dc2tog, 1dc in each of next 9 sts. (20 sts)

Round 38: Dc2tog, 1dc in each of next 8 sts, dc2tog, 1dc in each of next 8 sts. (18 sts)

Round 39: Dc2tog, 1dc in each of next 7 sts, dc2tog, 1dc in each of next 7 sts. (16 sts)

Stuff doll.

Round 40: Dc2tog around until hole closes.

Fasten off.

face

Using 3mm (D/3) hook and B, make 2ch.

Round 1: 6dc into second ch from hook. (6 sts)

Round 2: 2dc in each st. (12 sts)

Round 3: *1dc in next st, 2dc in next st; rep from * to end. (18 sts)

Round 4: *1dc in next 2 sts, 2dc in next st; rep from * to end. (24 sts)

Ss into next st and fasten off.

Sew in ends and press face. Using D, embroider two French knots for eyes and embroider mouth. Stitch face onto doll. Follow making-up instructions at end to complete doll.

medium doll body

Using 4mm (F/5) hook and D, make 2ch.

Round 1: 6dc into second ch from hook. (6 sts)

Round 2: 2dc in each st. (12 sts)

Round 3: *1dc in next st, 2dc in next st; rep from * to end. (18 sts)

Round 4: *1dc in each of next 2 sts, 2dc in next st; rep from * to end. (24 sts)

Round 5: *1dc in each of next 3 sts, 2dc in next st; rep from * to end. (30 sts)

Round 6: *1dc in each of next 4 sts, 2dc in next st; rep from * to end. (36 sts)

Rounds 7–8: 1dc in each st. (36 sts)

Change to E.

Rounds 9–11: 1dc in each st. (36 sts)

Round 12: Dc2tog, 1dc in each of next 16 sts, dc2tog, 1dc in each of next 16 sts. (34 sts)

Round 13: Dc2tog, 1dc in each of next 15 sts, dc2tog, 1dc in each of next 15 sts. (32 sts)

Round 14: Dc2tog, 1dc in each of next 14 sts, dc2tog, 1dc in each of next 14 sts. (30 sts)

Round 15: Dc2tog, 1dc in each of next 13 sts, dc2tog, 1dc in each of next 13 sts. (28 sts)

Round 16: Dc2tog, 1dc in each of next 12 sts, dc2tog, 1dc in each of next 12 sts. (26 sts)

Round 17: Dc2tog, 1dc in each of next 11 sts, dc2tog, 1dc in each of next 11 sts. (24 sts)

Round 18: 1dc in each st. (24 sts)

Change to F. Work next round in reverse dc.

Round 19: 1 reverse dc, *make 5ch, 1dc (standard) in second ch from hook, 1dc (standard) in next 4 ch, ss in next st; rep from * once more (headscarf ties). Cont in reverse dc to end. (24 sts)

Stop working in reverse dc and cont in standard dc.

Round 20: 1dc into the back of each st in E from Round 18 to end. (24 sts)

Round 21: Dc2tog, 1dc in each of next 10 sts, dc2tog, 1dc in each of next 10 sts. (22 sts)

Round 22: 1dc in each st. (22 sts)

Round 23: Dc2tog, 1dc in each of next 9 sts, dc2tog, 1dc in each of next 9 sts. (20 sts)

Round 24: Dc2tog, 1dc in each of next 8 sts, dc2tog, 1dc in each of next 8 sts. (18 sts)

Round 25: Dc2tog, 1dc in each of next 7 sts, dc2tog, 1dc in each of next 7 sts. (16 sts)

Stuff doll.

Round 26: Dc2tog around until hole closes.

Fasten off

face

Using 3mm (D/3) hook and G, make 2ch.

Round 1: 6dc into second ch from hook. (6 sts)

Round 2: 2dc in each st. (12 sts)

Round 3: *1dc in next st, 2dc in next st; rep from * to end. (18 sts)
Ss into next st and fasten off.

Sew in ends and press face. Using black embroidery thread, embroider two French knots for eyes and using red embroidery thread embroider mouth. Stitch face onto doll. Follow making-up instructions at end to complete doll.

small doll body
Using 4mm (F/5) hook and H, make 2ch.
Round 1: 6dc into second ch from hook. (6 sts)
Round 2: 2dc in each st. (12 sts)
Round 3: *1dc in next st, 2dc in next st; rep from * to end. (18 sts)
Round 4: *1dc in each of next 2 sts, 2dc in next st; rep from * to end. (24 sts)
Rounds 5-6: 1dc in each st. (24 sts)
Change to I.
Rounds 7-9: 1dc in each st. (24 sts)
Round 10: Dc2tog, 1dc in each of next 10 sts, dc2tog, 1dc in each of next 10 sts. (22 sts)
Round 11: 1dc in each st. (22 sts)
Round 12: Dc2tog, 1dc in each of next 9 sts, dc2tog, 1dc in each of next 9 sts. (20 sts)
Round 13: 1dc in each st. (20 sts)
Change to J. Work next round in reverse dc.
Round 14: 9 reverse dc, *make 3ch, 1dc (standard) in second ch from hook, 1dc (standard) in next 2 ch, ss in next st; rep from * once more (headscarf ties). Cont in reverse dc to end. (20 sts)
Stop working in reverse dc and cont in standard dc.
Round 15: 1dc into the back of each st in I from Round 13 to end. (20 sts)
Round 16: Dc2tog, 1dc in each of next 8 sts, dc2tog, 1dc in each of next 8 sts. (18 sts)
Round 17: Dc2tog, 1dc in each of next 7 sts, dc2tog, 1dc in each of next 7 sts. (16 sts)
Round 18: Dc2tog, 1dc in each of next 6 sts, dc2tog, 1dc in each of next 6 sts. (14 sts)
Round 19: Dc2tog, 1dc in each of next 5 sts, dc2tog, 1dc in each of next 5 sts. (12 sts)
Stuff doll.
Round 20: Dc2tog around until hole closes.
Fasten off.

face
Using 3mm (D/3) hook and K, make 2ch.
Round 1: 6dc into second ch from hook. (6 sts)
Round 2: 2dc in each st. (12 sts)
Ss into next st and fasten off.

Sew in ends and press face. Using black embroidery thread, embroider two French knots for eyes and using red embroidery thread embroider mouth. Stitch face onto doll. Follow making-up instructions at end to complete doll.

tiny doll body
Using 3.5mm (E/4) hook and L, make 2ch.
Round 1: 6dc into second ch from hook. (6 sts)
Round 2: 2dc in each st. (12 sts)
Round 3: *1dc in next st, 2dc in next st; rep from * to end. (18 sts)
Round 4: 1dc in each st. (18 sts)
Change to M.
Rounds 5–8: 1dc in each st. (18 sts)
Round 9: Dc2tog, 1dc in each of next 7 sts, dc2tog, 1dc in each of next 7 sts. (16 sts)
Round 10: 1dc in each st. (16 sts)
Change to N. Work next round in reverse dc.
Round 11: 9 reverse dc, *make 3ch, 1dc (standard) in second ch from hook, 1dc (standard) in next 2 ch, ss in next st; rep from * once more (headscarf ties). Cont in reverse dc to end. (16 sts)
Stop working in reverse dc and cont in standard dc.
Round 12: 1dc into the back of each stitch in M from Round 10 to end. (16 sts)
Round 13: Dc2tog, 1dc in each of next 6 sts, dc2tog, 1dc in each of next 6 sts. (14 sts)
Stuff doll.
Round 14: Dc2tog, 1dc in each of next 5 sts, dc2tog, 1dc in each of next 5 sts. (12 sts)
Round 15: Dc2tog, 1dc in each of next 4 sts, dc2tog, 1dc in each of next 4 sts. (10 sts)
Round 16: Dc2tog around until hole closes.
Fasten off.

face
Using 3mm (D/3) hook and O, make 2ch.
Round 1: 6dc into second ch from hook. (6 sts)
Round 2: 2dc in each st. (12 sts)
Ss into next st and fasten off.

Sew in ends and press face. Using black embroidery thread, embroider two French knots for eyes and using red embroidery thread embroider mouth. Stitch face onto doll. Follow making-up instructions at end to complete doll.

to make up (all dolls)
Sew headscarf ties in place. Sew hair in place by threading a wool or tapestry needle with hair colour and making large stitches from top of doll's head to sides. Embroider flowers and leaves onto doll or sew crochet flowers in place.

crochet flowers
Make several for each doll, each in two colours.
Using size 3mm (D/3) hook and first flower colour, make 4ch, join with ss to form a ring.
Make 5dc into the ring, join with ss.
Change colour.
Ss in first st, *2ch, 1htr, 2ch, ss in same st, ss into next st; rep from * 4 more times.
Fasten off.

Cherub Dress

Crochet dresses look very cute on little girls. The wool used for this dress has been hand-dyed, but you can use any 4 ply wool. If you'd like a larger size use (DK) double knit wool and larger hooks.

level 3: Enthusiast

materials
Natural Dye Studio Dazzle 4 ply (100% wool)
2 x 100g hanks (360m/394yds) Mimosa
4mm (F/5), 4.5mm (G/6), 5mm (H/8), and 5.5mm (I/9) crochet hooks
Yarn sewing needle
1m x 1cm (½in) wide ribbon
2 x small buttons

abbreviations
beg beginning
ch chain
dc double crochet
dec decrease/decreasing
dtr double treble
htr half treble
rem remaining
RS right side
ss slip stitch
st(s) stich(es)
tr treble

finished measurement
To fit a child 18 - 24 months old

tension
20dc x 15 rows over 10cm (4in) square, using 4mm (F/5) hook.

method
dress bodice
Begin at lower edge of front and back.
Using 4mm (F/5) hook, make 116ch.
Row 1 (RS): 1htr into third ch from hook, 1htr in each ch to end, 2ch, turn.
(work should now measure approx 58 - 61cm/23 - 24in. Use a smaller size hook if it's too long or a larger size hook if it's too short).

Divide for left front bodice:
Row 1: 1htr in next st and each of next 23 sts, 2ch, turn.
Row 2: Miss 1 st (counts as 1 dec at armhole edge), 1htr into next st and into each st to end, 2ch, turn.
Row 3: 1htr in each st to last 2 sts, miss 1 st, 1htr into last st (makes 1 dec at armhole edge), 2ch, turn.
Row 4: Rep Row 3 (makes 1 dec at front edge).
Row 5: Rep Row 2 (makes 1 dec at front edge).
Rep Rows 4 and 5, dec 1 st at front edge on every row until 11 sts rem.
Work straight if necessary until work measures 12.5cm (5in) above the first row of armhole edging.

Fasten off.

back bodice

Miss 10 sts on first Row 1 for left underarm, join yarn into next st.

Row 1: 2ch, 1htr into same st as joining st, 1htr into each of next 45 sts, 2ch, turn.

Row 2: 1htr into each st across (46 sts), 2ch, turn.

Rep Row 2 until work measures same as left front bodice.

Fasten off.

right front bodice

Miss next 10 sts on first Row 1 for right underarm, join yarn into next st.

Row 1: 2ch, 1htr into same st as joining st, 1htr into each rem st, 2ch, turn.

Work as left front bodice, starting at Row 2 and reversing shaping.

Fasten off.

skirt

Turn bodice upside down and work on original chain sts.

Using 4mm (F/5) hook and with RS facing, join yarn into first ch at beginning of left front 1ch.

Round 1: 1dc into joining st, 1dc into each ch to last ch of right front, join with a ss into first dc to form a circle. Put marker in loop on hook to mark beg of next round.

Round 2: 5ch, *miss next st, 1dtr into next st, 1ch; rep from * to end of round, ss into fourth of first 5ch. (57 spaces)

Round 3: 1ch, 1dc into same st as ss from previous round *1dc in next ch sp, 1dc into top of dtr from previous round; rep from * ending with 1dc in last ch sp, join with ss into first st. (114 sts)

Fasten off.

Divide for back skirt:

Change to 4.5mm (G/6) hook, rejoin yarn in middle of left armhole and

work on next 57 sts (this brings you to middle of right armhole).

Row 1: 2ch, 1dc into each of next 3 sts, *3ch, miss 3 sts, 1dc into next st; rep from * to last 3 sts, 1dc into each st, turn.

Row 2: 2ch, 1htr into each of next 3 sts, *1htr, 1tr, 1htr into 3ch sp; rep from * to last 3 sts, 1htr into each st, turn.

Row 3: 2ch, 1htr into next 3 sts, *3ch, miss (1htr, 1tr, 1htr), 1dc in next sp; rep from * to last 3 sts, 1htr into each st, turn.

Row 4: 2ch, 1htr into next 3 sts *1htr, 1tr, 1htr into ch sp; rep from * to last 3 sts, 1htr into each st, turn.

Row 5: 2ch, 1htr into next 3 sts *3ch, miss (1htr, 1tr, 1htr), 1dc into next sp; rep from * to last 3 sts, 1htr into each st, turn.

Row 6: 2ch, 1htr into first st, 2htr into next st, 1htr into next st, *1htr, 1tr, 1htr into next ch sp; rep from * to last 3 sts, 1htr into first st, 2htr into next st, 1htr into last st, turn.

Row 7: 2ch, 1htr into next 4 sts, *3ch, miss (1htr, 1tr, 1htr), 1dc into next sp; rep from * to last 4 sts, 1htr into each st, turn.

Row 8: 2ch, 1htr into next 4 sts, *1htr, 1tr, 1htr into next ch sp; rep from * to last 4 sts, 1htr into each st, turn.

Row 9: 2ch, 1htr into next 4 sts, *3ch, miss (1htr, 1tr, 1htr), 1dc into next sp: rep from * to last 4 sts, 1htr into each st, turn.

Row 10: 2ch, 1htr into first st, 2htr into next st, 1htr into next 2 sts, *1htr, 1tr, 1htr into next ch sp; rep from * to last 4 sts, 1htr into each of next 2 sts, 2htr into next st, 1htr, turn.

Row 11: 1ch, 1dc into next 2 sts, 3ch, miss 2 sts, 1dc into next space, *3ch, 1dc into next sp; rep from * to last 5 sts, 3ch, miss 2 sts, 1dc into next 3 sts, turn.

Change to 5mm (H/8) hook.

Row 12: 2ch, 1htr into first 3 sts, *1htr, 1tr, 1htr into each ch sp; rep from * to last 3 sts, 1htr into next 3 sts, turn.

Row 13: 1ch, 1dc into next 3 sts, *3ch, 1dc into next sp; rep from * to last 3 sts, 1dc into each st, turn.

Rows 14–17: Rep Rows 12–13 twice more.

Row 18: 2ch, 1htr into first st, 2htr into next st, 1htr into each of next 2 sts, *1htr, 1tr, 1htr into each ch sp; rep from * to last 4 sts, 1htr into each of next 2 sts, 2htr into next st, 1htr into last st, turn.

Row 19: 1ch, 1dc into next 3 sts, 3ch, miss 2 sts, 1dc into next st, *3ch, miss next 3 sts, 1dc into next sp; rep from * to last 5 sts, 3ch, miss 2 sts, 1dc into next 3 sts, turn.

Row 20: 2ch, 1htr into next 3 sts, *1htr, 1tr, 1htr into ch sp; rep from * to last 3 sts, 1htr into last 3 sts, turn.

Row 21: 1ch, 1dc into first 3 sts, *3ch, 1dc into sp; rep from * to last 3 sts, 1dc into last 3 sts, turn.

Rows 22–25: Rep Rows 20–21 twice more.

Row 26: 2ch, 1htr into next st, 2htr into next st, 1htr into next st, *1htr, 1tr, 1htr into each ch sp; rep from * to last 3 sts, 1htr into next st, 2htr into next st, 1htr into last st, turn.
Row 27: 1ch, 1dc into next 4 sts, *3ch, 1dc into next sp; rep from * to last 4 sts, 1dc into each st.
Change to 5.5mm (I/9) hook.
Row 28: 2ch, 1htr into next 4 sts, *1htr, 1tr, 1htr into each ch sp; rep from * to last 4 sts, 1htr into each st.
Row 29: 1ch, 1dc into next 4 sts, *3ch, 1dc into next sp; rep from * to last 4 sts, 1dc into each st.
Rows 30–39: Rep Rows 28–29 five times.
Fasten off.

front skirt
With RS facing, rejoin yarn at right side underarm, using 4.5mm (G/6) hook and work as for back.

to make up
Sew shoulder seams using an overstitch.

armhole edging
Using 4.5mm (G/6) hook, make both armhole edgings the same. With RS facing, join yarn at centre of underarm edge.
Round 1: Dc around armhole edge, join with a ss into first dc.
Round 2: 1ch, 1dc into same st as joining st, 1dc in each of next 2 sts, *3ch, 1dc in last dc made (picot made), 1dc in each of next 3 sts; rep from * around, join with ss into first dc.

Fasten off.

front and neck edging
Work in rows using 4.5mm (G/6) hook. With RS facing, join yarn at bottom centre of right front.
Row 1: Dc evenly up front edge, around neck and down left front edge (do not join).
Fasten off.
With RS facing, join yarn in first st on right front.
Row 2: 1ch, 1dc in joining st, 1dc in each of next 2 sts, *3ch, 1dc in last dc made (picot made), 1dc in each of next 2 sts; rep from * around right front, neck and down left side.
Fasten off.

Sew button onto left-hand side, corresponding with buttonhole (use the picot edging as button fasteners). Sew side seams together.

bottom edging
Starting with RS facing and at right-hand bottom edge (working upside down), and using 5.5mm (I/9) hook, rejoin yarn into a 3-ch sp. Make 1tr, 5dtr, 1tr into each 3ch sp around bottom of front and back edge. Join at end with a ss into top of first tr and fasten off.
Sew in ends.

Mrs Mittens Purse

This little purse will make any small child happy; it has a handy strap that goes around the neck so it can't be lost and is perfect for pocket money.

level 3: Enthusiast

materials

Rooster Almerino DK (50% baby alpaca, 50% merino wool)
1 x 50g ball (112.5m/124yds) 201 Cornish
4.5mm (G/6) crochet hook
Pair safety eyes
Fabric for purse lining
Sewing needle and thread
10cm (4in) zip
Fibrefill stuffing
Pink and black felt for muzzle
Embroidery threads for face and flower details
Yarn sewing needle

abbreviations

beg beginning
ch chain
dc double crochet
rep repeat
RS right side
st(s) stitches
WS wrong side

finished measurement

Approx 15cm (6in) diameter

tension

Tension is not critical on this project.

method

back of head

Round 1: Make 2ch, 6dc in second ch from hook. (*6 sts*)
Place st marker at beg of each round (when counting, loop on hook counts as one st).
Round 2: 2dc in each st. (*12 sts*)
Round 3: *1dc in next st, 2dc in next st; rep from * to end. (*18 sts*)
Round 4: *1dc in next 2 sts, 2dc in next st; rep from * to end. (*24 sts*)
Round 5: *1dc in next 3 sts, 2dc in next st; rep from * to end. (*30 sts*)
Round 6: *1dc in next 4 sts, 2dc in next st; rep from * to end. (*36 sts*)
Round 7: *1dc in next 5 sts, 2dc in next st; rep from * to end. (*42 sts*)
Round 8: *1dc in next 6 sts, 2dc in next st; rep from * to end. (*48 sts*)
Round 9: *1dc in next 7 sts, 2dc in next st; rep from * to end. (*54 sts*)
Round 10: *1dc in next 8 sts, 2dc in next st; rep from * to end. (*60 sts*)
Round 11: *1dc in next 9 sts, 2dc in next st; rep from * to end. (*66 sts*)
Round 12: *1dc in next 10 sts, 2dc in next st; rep from * to end. (*72 sts*)
Round 13: 1dc in each st.
Fasten off with a long tail approx 15cm (6in). Sew in ends.

lining

Cut two circles of lining fabric same size as crocheted pieces, plus 1.5cm (⅝in) extra all around for seam allowance. Insert zip by sewing either side to WS of lining circles. Turn through, so RS of lining is to inside. Sew lining together in a circle between zip ends. Sew two crochet circles RS together leaving side open for zip. Turn through and put purse lining inside crochet purse. Sew the open edges of the crochet circles along the zip to secure.

face

Round 1: Make 2ch, 6dc in second ch from hook. (*6 sts*)
Place st marker at beg of each round (when counting, loop on hook counts as one st).
Round 2: 2dc in each st. (*12 sts*)
Round 3: *1dc, 2dc; rep from * to end. (*18 sts*)
Round 4: *1dc in next 2 sts, 2dc; rep from * to end. (*24 sts*)
Round 5: *1dc in next 3 sts, 2dc; rep from * to end. (*30 sts*)
Rounds 6–7: 1dc in each st (this forms Mrs Mittens' nose).

Round 8: *1dc in next 4 sts, 2dc; rep from * to end. (*36 sts*)
Round 9: *1dc in next 5 sts, 2dc; rep from * to end. (*42 sts*)
Round 10: *1dc in next 6 sts, 2dc: rep from * to end. (*48 sts*)
Round 11: *1dc in next 7 sts, 2dc: rep from * to end. (*54 sts*)
Round 12: *1dc in next 8 sts, 2dc: rep from * to end. (*60 sts*)
Round 13: *1dc in next 9 sts, 2dc: rep from * to end. (*66 sts*)
Rounds 14–15: 1dc in each st.
Fasten off.

to make up

Insert eyes in place and secure. Crochet or sew face section onto front of purse, leaving seam open to allow for stuffing. Stuff lightly, filling nose section. Crochet or sew seam closed.

ears (make 2)

Make 10 ch.
Round 1: 1dc in 2nd st from hook, 1dc in each ch to end. (*9 sts*)
Round 2: 1 ch, 1dc in each dc.
Rep Row 2 until work forms a square. Fold square in half to form triangle and dc sides together; at top point make 2dc.
Fasten off. Pin and sew to head.

face detail

Embroider flower above one eye. Cut small felt circle for muzzle and felt triangle for nose. Sew nose to muzzle. Embroider mouth detail and sew muzzle to face. Embroider whiskers.

strap

Make 101ch (or adjust length to suit).
1dc in second ch from hook, 1dc in each ch to end.
Fasten off and sew ends to either side of purse near ears.

Summer Evening Shawl

This is a delightful light shawl, made with a simple diamond chain stitch, and is a great project to try when you have mastered a few skills.

level 3: Enthusiast

materials

Manos del Uruguay Lace (75% baby alpaca, 20% silk, 5% cashmere)
3 x 50g hanks (1200m/1320yds) 6977 Fay
3.5mm (E/4) crochet hook

abbreviations

beg beginning
ch chain
ch sp chain space
cont continue
dc double crochet
dtr double treble
st(s) stitch(es)
ss slip stitch

finished measurement

One size, approx 170 x 70cm (67 x 27½in)

tension

Tension is not critical on this project.

method

Make 202ch.

Row 1: 1dc in second chain from hook, *7ch, miss 3ch, ss in next ch; rep from * to end, make 9ch, turn.

Row 2: *ss in third ch in centre of first 7-ch arch, 7ch; rep from * across row ending with ss in third ch of last arch, 2ch, work 1dtr in last st, 8ch, turn.

Row 3: Ss in third ch of first 7-ch arch, *7ch, ss in third ch of next arch; rep from * across, 9ch, turn.

Rep Rows 2 and 3 until work measures approx 162cm (64in).

Fasten off.

picot edging

Place st marker at beg of each round.

Round 1: Join yarn into any st and place st marker. Work a complete round of dc, making 4dc into each side and finished edge loops and 1dc into each chain of cast-on edge. Work 3dc into each corner st to make the corners square. To join round, make ss into first dc.

Round 2: Work another round of dc, working 1dc into each of foundation row st and 3dc into each corner st. Make 2ch, ss into first dc from previous round.

Round 3: Rep Round 2.

Round 4: 6ch, miss next 2 sts, 1dc in next st, *3ch, miss next 2 sts, 1dc in next st; rep from * to end (cont to work 3dc into corner st as previous rows).

Round 5: 1ch, ss in first 3ch sp, *6ch, ss in fourth ch from hook, 2ch, ss in next 3ch sp; rep from * to end.

Fasten off and sew in ends.

Pavlova

This crochet dessert looks so yummy, you'll just want to eat it! You could also use the fruit to trim other items.

level 3: Enthusiast

materials

Rooster Almerino DK (50% baby alpaca, 50% merino wool)
1 x 50g ball (112.5m/124yds) each of:
202 Hazelnut (A)
201 Cornish (B)
207 Gooseberry (E)
Rowan Pure Wool DK (100% superwash wool)
1 x 50g ball (125m/137yds) 028 Raspberry (C)
Debbie Bliss Rialto DK (100% extra-fine merino wool)
1 x 50g ball (105m/114yds) 15 Deep Purple (D)

3mm (D/3) crochet hook
Yarn sewing needle
Fibrefill stuffing

abbreviations

ch chain
dc double crochet
dec decrease
foll following
htr half treble
rem remaining
RS right side
st(s) stitch(es)
ss slip stitch
tr treble
yrh yarn round hook

special abbreviation

cl (cluster) dc into first st, leaving last loop of each st on hook. *5dtr into next st, yarn round hook and draw through all loops on hook (1 cluster).

finished measurement

Approx 13cm (5in) diameter

tension

Tension is not critical on this project.

method

base

Using A, make 4ch, join with ss to form a ring.
Round 1: 12dc into ring, ss into first ch.
Round 2: 1ch, 2dc into same place as 1ch, 2dc into each st of previous round, ss into top of first st. (24 *sts*)
Round 3: 1ch, 1dc into each st to end, ss into top of first st. (24 *sts*)
Round 4: 1ch, 2dc into first st, 1dc into next st, *2dc into next st, 1dc into next st; rep from * to end, ss into first st. (36 *sts*)
Round 5: Rep Round 3. (36 *sts*)
Round 6: 1ch, 2dc into first st, *1dc into each of next 2 sts, 2dc into next st; rep from * to last 2 sts, 1dc into each st, ss into top of first st. (48 *sts*)
Round 7: Rep Round 3. (48 *sts*)
Round 8: 1ch, 2dc into first st, *1dc into each of next 3 sts, 2dc into next st; rep from * to last 3 sts, 1dc into each st, ss into first st. (60 *sts*)
Round 9: Rep Round 3. (60 *sts*)
Round 10: 1ch, 2dc into first st, *1dc into each of next 4 sts, 2dc into next st; rep from * to last 4 sts, 1dc into each st, ss into first st. (72 *sts*)
Round 11: Rep Round 3. (72 *sts*)
Round 12: 1ch, 2dc into first st, *1dc into each of next 5 sts, 2dc into next st; rep from * to last 5 sts, 1dc into each st, ss into first st. (84 *sts*)
Round 13: Rep Round 3. (84 *sts*)

Side edging:
Using A, 1ch.
Round 1: 1dc into each st (working into back loop only) to end, ss into first st. (84 *sts*)
Round 2: 1ch, dc2tog, *1dc into next 5 sts, dc2tog; rep from * to last 5 sts, 1dc into each st, ss into first st. (72 *sts*)
Round 3: 1dc into each st, ss into first st. (72 *sts*)

top

Using A, work Rounds 1–12 from base pattern.
Fasten off.

cream frill

Using B, make 48ch, ss into first ch to form a ring.
Round 1: 1ch, 1dc into each st, ss into first st.
Work the foll two rounds into back loop of each st only.
Round 2: 2ch, 1htr into same place as 2ch, 2htr into each dc of previous round, ss into top of first 2-ch.
Round 3: 3ch, 1tr into same place as 3ch, 3tr into each htr of previous round, ss into top of first 3-ch.
Work into top 2 loops of each st.
Round 4: 1ch, 1dc into same place as 1ch, 1dc in each tr from previous round, ss into first st.
Fasten off.

raspberries (Make 5 in C, 5 in D)

Make 4ch, join with ss to form a ring.
Round 1: 8dc into ring, ss into first st of previous round.
Round 2: 1ch, 2dc into each st, ss into first st. (16 sts)
Round 3: 1ch, 1dc into each st, ss into first st.
Round 4: Rep Round 3.
Round 5: 1ch, dc2tog, *dc2tog; rep from * 6 more times, ss into first st.
Roll small amount of stuffing into ball and place inside raspberry.
Round 6: 1dc into each of rem 8 sts, ss into first st. Leave long length of yarn.
Fasten off.
Thread a yarn sewing needle with yarn and thread through all 8 sts, pull tight and secure.

grape centre

Using E, make 8ch.

Row 1: 1dc into second ch from hook, 1dc into each of foll 6ch, turn. (*7 sts*)

Row 2: 1ch, cl, 1dc into next st; rep from * once more, turn. (*3 clusters*).

Row 3: 1ch, 2dc into first st, *1dc into top of cluster, 1dc into next st; rep from * to last st, 2dc into last st.

Row 4: 1ch, 1dc into first st, (1cl into next st, 1dc into next st) 4 times, turn. (*4 clusters*)

Rep Rows 3 and 4 once more. (*5 clusters*).

Row 7: 1ch, miss first st, 1dc into each of next 9 sts, turn. (*2 sts dec*)

Row 8: 1ch, 1dc into first st, *1cl into next st, dc into next st; rep from * to end. (*4 clusters*)

Rep Rows 7 and 8 once more, ending with 3 clusters.

Fasten off.

individual grapes

Using E, make 4ch, miss 3ch, into next ch make 4dtr cluster (same as for grape centre), pull yarn tight so that cluster forms a smooth dome on RS, make 3ch, ss into base of cluster.

Fasten off.

to make up

With base facing, place top on base and overstitch in place one row below top seam. Sew approx three-quarters of the way around, place stuffing inside and complete sewing up. Place cream frill on top of pavlova base and sew in place. Place raspberries on top of cream frill edge, alternating between dark and mid pink. Sew in place. With grape centre facing, sew on the six grapes randomly to form a small dome. Place grape dome on centre of pavlova and sew in place.

Felted Cherry Brooch

These cherries are very quick and really cute. They are Improver level because they are small and so a little more fiddly, but the stitch is very simple – so once you've mastered crocheting in the round, give them a go. To felt well, they must be made in 100% wool.

level 2: Improver

materials

Cascade 220 DK (100% Peruvian wool)
1 x 100g hank (200m/220yds) each of:
8414 Bright Red (A)
0980 Pesto (B)
3.5mm (E/4) crochet hook
Yarn sewing needle
Small brooch clip

abbreviations

ch chain
dc double crochet
htr half treble
st(s) stitch(es)
ss slip stitch

finished measurement

Approx 7cm (2¾ in) width x 7.5cm (3in) length

tension

Tension is not critical on this project.

method

cherries (make two)

Using A, make 2ch.
Round 1: 6dc in second ch from hook.
Round 2: 2dc in each st. (12 sts)
Round 3: 1dc in each st. (12 sts)
Stuff cherry with scraps of red wool.
Round 4: Dc2tog around. (6 sts)
Continue to dc2tog until hole closes.
Fasten off.
Sew in ends.

stalk (make one)

Using B, make 20ch.
Fasten off.

Leaves (make two)

Using B, make 8ch, ss in second ch from hook, 1dc, 1htr, 1tr, 1htr, 1dc, ss in last ch.
Working on other side of ch, ss in second ch from hook, 1dc in next st, 1htr, 1tr, 1htr, 1dc, ss.
Fasten off.

to make up

Sew one end of stalk to each cherry. Sew leaves to top of stalk. Wash in the washing machine on a hot wash, twice. Attach a brooch pin to back of leaves, so that you can't see it from the front.

Monty and Priscilla Bear

Although these gorgeous teddies are made using double crochet, which is the most basic stitch, it's in the Enthusiast level because there is a lot of counting during the making. The secret is to count at the end of each round and mark your rounds with a marker; I use a piece of contrasting yarn, or you can buy ready-made stitch markers.

level 3: Enthusiast

materials
teddy 1
Rooster Almerino DK (50% baby alpaca, 50% merino wool)
2 x 50g balls (225m/248yds) 205 Glace

teddy 2
Rooster Almerino DK (50% baby alpaca, 50% merino wool)
2 x 50g balls (225m/248yds) 203 Strawberry Cream

3.5mm (E/4) crochet hook
Pair safety eyes
Fibrefill stuffing
Yarn needle
Brown yarn for face details
Ribbon for bow or headband

abbreviations
ch chain
dc double crochet
dc2tog Insert hook into next st, draw a loop through, insert hook into next st, draw a loop through, pull through all 3 sts.
rep repeat
st(s) stitch(es)
ss slip stitch
WS wrong side

finished measurement
Approx 31cm (12in) high

tension
Tension is not critical on this project.

method
head
Round 1: Make 2ch, 6dc in second ch from hook. (6 *sts*)
Place st marker at beg of each round (when counting, loop on hook counts as one st).
Round 2: 2dc in each st. (12 *sts*)
Round 3: *1dc in first st, 2dc in next st; rep from * to end. (18 *sts*)
Rounds 4–5: 1dc in each st.
Round 6: *1dc in next 2 sts, 2dc in next st: rep from * to end. (24 *sts*)
Rounds 7–8: 1dc in each st. (24 *sts*)
Round 9: 1dc in next 7 sts, 2dc in next 10 sts, 1dc in next 7 sts. (34 *sts*)
Round 10: *1dc in next st, 2dc in next st; rep from * once more, 1dc in next 25 sts, 2dc in next st, 1dc in next 2 sts, 2dc in next st, 1dc. (38 *sts*)
Round 11: 1dc in next 11 sts, 2dc in next st, *1dc in next 2 sts, 2dc in next st; rep from * 4 times more, 1dc in next 11 sts. (44 *sts*)
Round 12-18: 1dc in each st. (44 *sts*)
Round 19: 1dc, dc2tog, 1dc in next 2 sts, dc2tog, 1dc in next 30 sts, dc2tog, 1dc in next 2 sts, dc2tog, 1dc. (40 *sts*)
Round 20: 1dc in next 11 sts, dc2tog, 1dc in next 2 sts, dc2tog, 1dc in next 6 sts, dc2tog, 1dc in next 2 sts, dc2tog, 1dc in next 11 sts. (36 *sts*)
Round 21: 1dc in each st. (36 *sts*)
Round 22: *1dc in next 4 sts, dc2tog: rep from * to end. (30 *sts*)
Round 23: *1dc in next 3 sts, dc2tog: rep from * to end. (24 *sts*)
Insert eyes approx 9 or 10 rows from nose and stuff head.
Round 24: *1dc in next 2 sts, dc2tog; rep from * to end. (18 *sts*)
Round 25: *1dc in next st, dc2tog; rep from * to end. (12 *sts*)
Round 26: Dc2tog around. (6 *sts*)
Fasten off with a long tail approx 15cm (6in). Finish stuffing head, then use yarn needle to thread tail through sts of last round to close gap neatly. Sew in ends.

ears (make 4)
(do not count loop on hook as one st on this section – st marker is not necessary)
Make 2ch, 6dc in second ch from hook (do not join ring), turn. (6 *sts*)
Row 1: 1ch, 1dc in next st, make 2dc in next 4 sts, 1dc. (10 *sts*)
Row 2: 1ch, 2dc in first st, *1dc in next 2 sts, 2dc in next st; rep from * twice more. (14 *sts*)
Fasten off.

body

Place st marker at beginning of each round.

Round 1: 2ch, 6dc in second ch from hook, join round and each subsequent round with ss. (6 sts)

Round 2: 2dc in each st. (12 sts)

Round 3: *2dc in first st, 1dc in next st; rep from * to end. (18 sts)

Round 4: *2dc in first st, 1dc in next 2 sts; rep from * to end. (24 sts)

Rounds 5–7: 1dc in each st. (24 sts)

Round 8: 1dc in first st, 2dc in next st, *1dc in next 3 sts, 2dc in next st; rep from * to last 2 sts, 1dc in each st. (30 sts)

Rounds 9-10: 1dc in each st. (30 sts)

Round 11: *1dc in next 4 sts, 2dc in next st; rep from * to end. (36 sts)

Rounds 12–13: 1dc in each st (36 sts)

Round 14: *1dc in next 5 sts, 2dc in next st; rep from * to end. (42 sts)

Rounds 15–17: 1dc in each st. (42 sts)

Round 18: 1dc in next 8 sts, 2dc in next st, *1dc in next 4 sts, 2dc in next st; rep from * 4 times more, 1dc in each st to end. (48 sts)

Rounds 19–22: 1dc in each st. (48 sts)

Round 23: 1dc in next 3 sts, dc2tog, *1dc in next 6 sts, dc2tog; rep from * 4 times more, 1dc in each st. (42 sts)

Round 24: 1dc in each st. (42 sts)

Round 25: 1dc in next 4 sts, dc2tog, *1dc in next 9 sts, dc2tog; rep from * twice more, 1dc in next 3 sts. (38 sts)

Round 26: 1dc in next 3 sts, dc2tog, *1dc in next 8 sts, dc2tog, rep from * twice more, 1dc in next 3 sts. (34 sts)

Round 27: 1dc in next 3 sts, dc2tog, *1dc in next 7 sts, dc2tog; rep from * twice more, 1dc in next 2 sts. (30 sts)

Round 28: 1dc in each st. (30 sts)

Round 29: *1dc in next 3 sts, dc2tog; rep from * to end. (24 sts)

Stuff body.

Round 30: *1dc in next 2 sts, dc2tog; rep from * to end. (18 sts)

Round 31: *1dc in next st, dc2tog; rep from * to end. (12 sts)

Round 32: Dc2tog around. (6 sts)

Fasten off with a long tail approx 15cm (6in). Finish stuffing body and use yarn needle to thread tail through sts of last round to close gap neatly. Sew in ends.

legs (make two)

Round 1: 2ch, 6dc in second ch from hook.

Round 2: 2dc in each st. (12 sts)

Round 3: *2dc in first st, 1dc in next st; rep from * to end. (18 sts)

Round 4: *2dc in first st, 1dc in next 2 sts; rep from * to end. (24 sts)

Round 5-6: 1dc in each st. (24 sts)

Round 7: *Dc2tog, 1dc in next st; rep from * to end. (16 sts)

Round 8: 1dc in each st. (16 sts)

Rep Round 8 until work measures 12cm (4½in).

Fasten off. Sew in ends.

arms (make two)

Rep pattern as for legs.

Fasten off. Sew in ends.

to make up

Place two ears with WS together. Join yarn into one corner by pushing hook through both ears. 1ch, make 1dc around by pushing hook through both ears to join top of ears (semi-circle). Ss into bottom corner of semi-circle to join. Rep with other set of ears.

Fasten off. Sew in ends. Sew ears onto head.

Sew body to head with widest part at bottom. Stuff legs and arms and attach to body. Attach ribbon and tie in a bow around neck or head. Embroider nose and mouth onto face.

---

tips

Use very soft wool such as Rooster Almerino, which is a mix of alpaca and super-soft merino wool.

Safety eyes are best or embroider the eyes – even if you are not making this for a small child, it may eventually reach little hands or little mouths.

Do not over stuff; teddy should be lovely, soft and cuddly. When stuffing, break up the stuffing into small pieces before inserting into toy.

When sewing pieces together, always pin in place first to check that positioning looks correct.

UK suppliers

The yarns used in these projects should be available from your local yarn or craft store. If you can't find the correct yarn, try some of the websites listed here.

The Berwick Street Cloth Shop
Linings and trimmings
14 Berwick Street
London W1F 0PP
020 7287 2881
www.theberwickstreetclothshop.com

Blue Faced Yarn Shop
H W Hammand & Co
The Croft Stables
Station Lane
Great Barrow
Cheshire CH3 7JN
www.bluefaced.com

Dancing Hens Craft Studio
Wool, books and tuition
Battlers Green Farm
Radlett
Hertfordshire
WD7 8PH
01923 856619
www.dancinghens.com

Debbie Bliss Yarns
Designer Yarns
Units 8-10
Newbridge Industrial Estate
Pitt Street
Keighley
West Yorkshire BD21 4PQ
01535 664222
www.designeryarns.uk.com

Fyberspates
The Maintenance Room
The Nalder Estate
East Challow
Nr Wantage
Oxfordshire
OX12 9SY
07540 656660
www.fyberspates.co.uk

Ingrid Wagner
Giant crochet supplies
Studio 5
The Stone Barn
Kirkharle Courtyard
Kirkharle
Northumberland NE19 2PE
01830 540117
www.ingridwagner.com

John Lewis
Stores nationwide
0845 604 9049
www.johnlewis.com

Natural Dye Studio
Moors Farm
Hollesley
Woodbridge
Suffolk IP12 3RF
01394 411500
www.thenaturaldyestudio.com

Rooster Yarns
Laughing Hens online
Wool, patterns, knitting & crochet supplies
Online.
www.laughinghens.com
01829 740903

Rowan Yarns
Green Lane Mill
Holmfirth
West Yorkshire HD9 2DX
01484 681881
www.knitrowan.com

VV Rouleaux
Ribbons and trimmings
101 Marylebone Lane
London W1U 2QD
020 7224 5179
www.vvrouleaux.com

TUITION

Nicki Trench Workshops
Crochet, knitting, and craft workshops all levels
Email: nicki@nickitrench.com

US suppliers

YARN SUPPLIERS

Debbie Bliss
www.debbieblissonline.com

Coats Craft Rowan Yarns
www.coatscrafts.co.uk

Purl Soho
www.purlsoho.com

Yarn Forward
www.yarnforward.com

Fyberspates
www.fyberspates.co.uk

Rooster Yarns
www.laughinghens.com

Rooster & Fyberspates
Knitcellaneous
120 Acorn Street
Merlin,
OR 97532
www.knitcellaneous.com

Bluefaced Leicester
Wool2Dye4
6000-K Boonsboro Road
Coffee Crossing
Lynchburg
VA 24503
www.wool2dye4.com

STOCKISTS

A.C. Moore
Stores nationwide
1-888-226-6673
www.acmoore.com

Crafts, etc.
Online store
1-800-888-0321
www.craftsetc.com

Hobby Lobby
Stores nationwide
www.hobbylobby.com

Jo-Ann Fabric and Craft Store
Stores nationwide
1-888-739-4120
www.joann.com

Knitting Fever
Stockists of Debbie Bliss, Noro, and Sirdar yarns
www.knittingfever.com

Knitting Garden
Stockists of Rowan yarns
www.theknittinggarden.com

Laughing Hens
Wool, patterns, knitting & crochet suppliers
online
www.laughinghens.com

Lets Knit
www.letsknit.com

Michaels
Stores nationwide
1-800-642-4235
www.michaels.com

Unicorn Books and Crafts
www.unicornbooks.com

WEBS
www.yarn.com

Yarn Market
www.yarnmarket.com

Index

Acknowledgements

I love crochet and was delighted to be given the opportunity to be involved in a book where I could include all my favourite crochet things. Making this book has been hugely enjoyable on many levels and I'm so lucky to have worked with such an enthusiastic and talented team.

Thank you to all those at Cico, particularly Cindy Richards, Sally Powell and Pete Jorgensen for making my job easy by giving me such a gorgeous palette of colours to work with, beautiful artwork and great organisation. Also big thanks to Marie Clayton for her expert editing eye and crochet knowledge.

I'm indebted to my expert crocheters who helped enormously to get the projects finished in time for the deadlines: Emma Lightfoot, Tracey Elks, Julie Swinhoe, Michelle Bull, Zara Poole and Jenny Shore. Also thanks to Emma Fontaine for her help with the Russian Dolls and Jill Holden for her swift help in pattern checking at the last minute. Also thanks to my many Dancing Hens customers for their invaluable support and sanity checking of the projects. Also to Roger Perkins for coming up with the right words.

I'm also extremely grateful to the UK yarn companies who donated the yarn for the book, particularly to Andy and Johnny at Laughing Hens for the mounds of Rooster yarn; Jenny at Fyberspates, Designer Yarns for Debbie Bliss yarns and to Rowan Yarns for the Amy Butler Belle yarns.

As ever, another huge thanks to my mother, who not only taught me everything I know about crochet but also contributed to making, designing and checking the projects in this book and who I couldn't do without.